WHERE TO GO
IN
TUNISIA

REG BUTLER

SETTLE PRESS
HIPPOCRENE BOOKS INC.

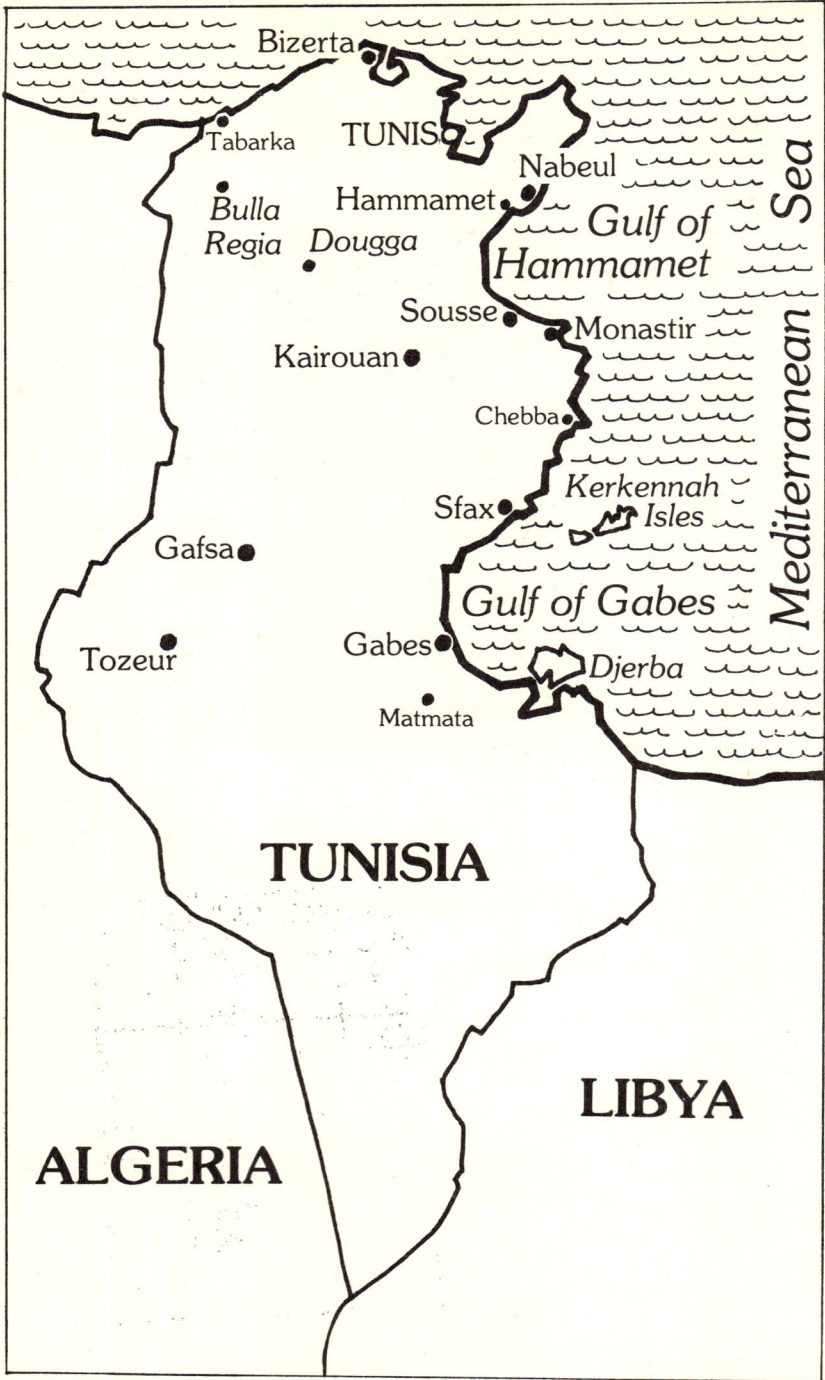

Bizerta

TUNIS

Tabarka

Nabeul

Bulla
Regia

Hammamet

*Gulf of
Hammamet*

Dougga

Sousse

Monastir

Kairouan

Chebba

*Kerkennah
Isles*

Sfax

Mediterranean Sea

Gafsa

Gulf of Gabes

Gabes

Djerba

Tozeur

Matmata

TUNISIA

LIBYA

ALGERIA

Foreword

As the leading holiday company operating in Tunisia, Thomson Holidays are happy to be associated with Reg Butler's new book 'Where To Go in Tunisia'.

From his early visits to the country, 40 years ago, the author has kept in close contact with the development of Tunisia into a major year-round Mediterranean destination for sun-seeking holidaymakers.

But Tunisia offers much more than golden beaches and good hotels. In this guide-book, Reg Butler shows you where to go and what to visit in this remarkable country of desert oases, Roman remains, and Arab towns and villages.

We are sure you will find this book invaluable in helping you plan your Tunisian holiday. Reg Butler's advice, tips and practical background information will ensure you get maximum sightseeing value from your stay in Tunisia.

Thomson Holidays

BEL		MAR		
BRD		NOF		
BGT		POC		
DRI		SKI		
ELL		SOU		
FLA		STB		
GIL		SWA		
HED	8/90	WIT		
HOR		MOB		
LEV		Coms		
LIT				

© 1990 Reg Butler
First published by Settle Press
10 Boyne Terrace Mews
London W11 3LR

Maps and Plans by Mary Butler

ISBN (Hardback) 0 907070 48 5
          (Paperback) 0 907070 49 3

Published in USA by Hippocrene Books Inc
171 Madison Avenue,
New York N.Y. 10016

ISBN 0-87052-721-5

Printed by Villiers Publications Ltd
26a Shepherds Hill, London N6 5AH

Contents

1. Sand, Sea and Sahara

There's no shortage of sand in North Africa, and Tunisia is now making the most of other holidaymaker attractions: year-round sunshine, low prices, modern purpose-built hotels and resorts. Thanks to the former French connection, cuisine and language is French everywhere, with children learning that language from primary school onwards. But that European-type background goes with 'different' sightseeing: Moslem cities, bazaars, oases, desert cave-dwellings and ancient Roman sites.

Most of the modern hotels are Moorish in design and furnishing, but low profile, no higher than tree level. They are built totally with European holidaymakers in mind, and facilities are of high standard. Within the hotel complex, you could be anywhere in the Mediterranean. From the middle price-range upwards, all have their own swimming pools; and most have their own beach frontage.

Tunisia is closer to Britain than Malta or Greece, and direct flights by charter or scheduled services now deliver you within 3 hours to Tunis, Monastir, Sfax or the Island of Djerba. From those airports you can easily reach the three main areas of tourism development.

Within a 90-minute drive of Tunis or Monastir is the resort of Hammamet, with soft white sand. Hotels are built in garden settings, outside the small walled city with its 15th-century Kasbah. Hammamet and neighbouring Nabeul were the first of Tunisia's resorts to be established, and are the nearest to the capital.

Nabeul is famous for its pottery. Friday is market day, when countrymen arrive with camels, donkeys and sheep, or set up luscious displays of fruit and vegetables.

Tunis itself is a city with white blocks of apartments, French-type bars and restaurants. But inside the Medina - the traditional Arab town - you can stroll through bazaars, which locally are called souks. Whole sections are devoted to the ancient crafts - brass-workers, slipper-makers, perfumers, dyers, potters, weavers, tanners. Tourists are welcome to watch. It's the Middle Ages come to life, nothing changed.

Since long before the present boom in tourism, the Tunisian government has fostered handicraft skills through special trade schools. It ensures that most traditional souvenirs are of good quality. Haggling is part of the fun.

A suburb of Tunis is the delightful village of Sidi-Bou-Said, with glittering white houses, blue doorways and grille-work windows.

Close by are the ruins of ancient Carthage. Over the centuries, Carthage has been exploited as a handy stone-quarry, and relatively little remains. But the Bardo museum in Tunis contains one of the world's best collections of Roman and Christian mosaics.

Halfway down the Tunisian coast, the well-established resorts of Sousse, Port El Kantaoui, Skanès, Monastir and Mahdia are served by direct charter flights to Monastir.

The most luxurious destination is Port El Kantaoui, rated as the St. Tropez of North Africa, just north of Sousse. There's all the usual access to watersports, horse or camel riding, or golf on a championship course dotted with palm, olive and pomegranate trees. Around the 340-boat marina are waterfront restaurants, boutiques and nightspots.

As Tunisia's third largest city, Sousse has a fascinating old quarter where visitors can shop for costume jewelry, brilliant handwoven blankets, cushion-covers and carved olive wood. This coastal region is fringed with large green plantations of olive trees.

Inland, 35 miles from Sousse, there's easy access to Kairouan - a holy city of Islam, with a long history as Tunisia's former capital. The Grand Mosque was founded in 670 AD by a follower of the prophet Mohammed, and has remained a place of major Islamic pilgrimage ever since. Kairouan is also Tunisia's leading carpet- and rug-making centre.

Coach or mini-bus trips can take you to Roman remains and - further south - to Sahara-type oases and the desert cave-dwellings of Matmata. The easily-reached Colosseum at El Djem can rival the similar monument in Rome with seating for 35,000, and better preserved.

Gabès is another world: a luxuriant oasis near the coast, with thousands of date-palms and a serene life-style. Visitors enjoy a change of pace, touring the oasis by horse-carriage. Alongside each plot of land is a precious rivulet of water, nourishing the dates, bananas, oranges and figs: a fruitarian's paradise.

Oases and cave-men can be reached on day trips from the blissful holiday island of Djerba - Homer's Island of the Lotus-Eaters - linked by a Roman-built causeway to the mainland. During recent years, the new beachside hotels have attracted an international clientele of sun-worshippers.

Outside the hotels, the way of life is little changed from centuries past. In Djerba's pottery village of Gueilala, craftsmen still use techniques that are quite unchanged since their potters' wheels first began to spin over 2,000 years ago.

The most incredible relic from the past is the desert cave village of Matmata, which was used as a 'Star Wars' location. After a journey into the hills, you look down onto a broad valley, pitted like the crater-scarred surface of the moon.

The easily-worked rock is shaped into a series of tunnels down to a courtyard pit that gives access to rooms and stables and store-rooms. Caves keep warm in winter, cool in summer. They are well protected against dust and sand-storms. Whitewashed rooms are furnished with niches, shelves and working surfaces hewn from the living rock.

For seeing first-hand yet another life-style, it's a great experience to continue your safari to the desert oases of Tozeur and Nefta. The route crosses the huge area of dried salt lakes called the Chotts, where the tantalising sight of a mirage is virtually guaranteed. From the oases you can ride in Lawrence of Arabia style by camel or jeep across shifting dunes of powder-fine sand.

Back in your 20th-century oasis hotel, cuisine still keeps the strong French influence from the hundred years of French occupation. The French inheritance has also left the country with a well-established wine production, and French as the main second language.

Take another look at a map of the Mediterranean. Tunisia is virtually dead centre - just across the water to Sicily, at the tip of Italy; and mostly north of Malta. So you can enjoy a pure Mediterranean-style holiday, with all the excitement of exploring the fringes of the Sahara in the south.

Tunisia is a year-round destination. Even during the December-February 'winter' you'll get temperatures that are better than May in Britain, with around five hours' daily sunshine - or even more in the South. That's ideal weather for sightseeing, Sea and Sahara in a day!

As you travel around, you'll catch scenes lifted straight from past centuries. Greybeards lean on their crooks, as they guard flocks of sheep and goats. In villages, women gossip at a well, and then saunter off with water-jug perched on their shoulder. Camels sneer at human beings as they lope into a local market. Traditional costume is everywhere.

Be discreet with your photography, and you'll return with pictures that are far more exotic than anything from the European shores of the Mediterranean. Pack a tape recorder, and you'll be able to remind yourself of all those evocative sound effects of Tunisia: the grumbling of camels, the frenzied sales patter of the markets, and the call of the muezzin awakening you every morning at 4.30 to welcome the dawn.

Resort Guide
The recipe for a perfect Tunisian holiday is spiced with different ingredients. The principal cities and resorts are given star ratings for ease of access, beaches, sightseeing and night-life. The overall Butler rating is a personal assessment on how these ingredients combine into a good mixture for an interesting holiday. But everyone to his own taste. Some folk may feel that total absence of night-life is a plus point, deserving five stars!

KEY

Flights
★★★★	airport with direct or connecting flight from Britain
★★★	an easy drive, between 1 and 2 hours from airport
★★	between 2 and 3 hours from airport
★	a long haul from the airport, at least 3 hours

Beaches
★★★★	excellent, with easy access
★★★	good, in the area
★★	scattered in coves
★	limited

Water sport - Yes, or No

Sites
★★★★ spectacular
★★★ several interesting sites to see
★★ one or two sites
★ within range, on day trips

Scenery
★★★★ superb
★★★ special
★★ good
★ average

Eating out
★★★★ excellent variety of food and restaurants
★★★ above-average choice of restaurants
★★ average
★ limited choice

Nightlife
★★★★ pulsating
★★★ plentiful
★★ average
★ Sleepy

Butler's Rating Tables

	Flights	Beaches	Water sport Y/N	Sites	Scenery	Eating out	Night life	Rating
Tunis	★★★★	★	N	★★★	★★	★★★★	★★	5
Hammamet	★★★	★★★★	Y	★★	★★	★★	★★	9
Nabeul	★★	★★★★	Y	★	★	★	★	6
Port el Kantaoui	★★★	★★★★	Y	★	★	★★★	★★	7
Sousse	★★★	★★★★	Y	★★	★	★★	★★	8
Skanès	★★★★	★★★★	Y	★★	-	★	★	6
Monastir	★★★★	★★★★	Y	★★	★	★	★	6
Mahdia	★★★	★★★	Y	★	★	★	★	4
Kerkennah	★	★★★★	Y	–	★	–	–	2
Djerba	★★★★	★★★★	Y	★★	★★	★★	★	6
Zarzis	★★	★★★★	Y	★	★	★	★	4

Which Sightseeing Guide

	Build-ings	Setting
CLASSICAL		
Dougga	8	6
Bulla Regia	5	5
Zaghouan	6	7
Thuburbo Majus	6	8
Sbeitla	7	4
Carthage	4	9
Makthar	6	7
El Djem	10	6
Kerkouane	2	7
Utica	2	4
ARAB		
Tunis	8	6
Sidi Bou Said	10	10
Hammamet	6	7
Kairouan	10	9
Sousse	8	7
Monastir	7	7
Mahdia	7	8
Sfax	6	5
THE SOUTH		
Gabès	2	9
Djerba	7	8
Matmata	10	10
Douz	3	5
Tozeur	8	9
Nefta	6	10
Tamerza	2	10
Chenini-Tataouine	8	8
Medenine	5	4

Temperatures - average daily maximum (°F)

	JAN	FEB	MAR	APR	MAY	JUN	JUL	AUG	SEP	OCT	NOV	DEC
Tunis	58	61	65	70	76	84	90	91	87	77	68	60
For comparison												
London	43	45	49	54	60	68	72	73	65	58	52	47

Hours of Daily Sunshine

	JAN	FEB	MAR	APR	MAY	JUN	JUL	AUG	SEP	OCT	NOV	DEC
Tunis	4.9	5.5	6.6	6.4	9.6	10.9	11.6	10.1	7.2	5.9	5.1	4.4
Tozeur	7.1	7.4	6.9	9.5	10.6	11.0	11.4	10.9	8.6	6.3	6.2	6.3
London	1.5	2.3	3.6	5.3	6.4	7.1	6.4	6.0	4.7	3.2	1.8	1.3

Average Sea Temperatures (°F)

JAN	FEB	MAR	APR	MAY	JUN	JUL	AUG	SEP	OCT	NOV	DEC
59	60	62	63	65	71	78	80	82	74	65	60

2. Choosing a Holiday

When to Go

Tunisia is a year-round destination, thanks to a climate which is pure Mediterranean along the coast; and African, inland and south. Temperatures range from mild in winter, to hot or fiendish during high summer in desert areas.

Rainfall is irregular, and varies widely according to season and region. Three-fourths of the annual rainfall comes during the cool 'winter' season. Average rainfall in the extreme north, near Tabarka, is over 60" a year; in the far south, barely 6" annually. That makes all the difference between cork-oak forests on mountain crests in the north, and total desert in the south.

The Cap Bon peninsula - the thumb that juts into the strategic centre of the Mediterranean, pointing at Sicily - is much greener than further south. The Hammamet-Nabeul area gets between 16" and 32" of rain, which comes mainly from October till late March in quick bursts, followed by a return to blue skies. Springtime is the season of most luxuriant growth. During summer, there's hardly any rain, but fairly high humidity. By September, the countryside is parched and dusty, thirsting for those winter downpours.

To summarise: there's lush countryside in the extreme northwest; bone-dry summers along the east-facing coast, with much less annual rainfall; and semi-arid areas inland, leading southwards to dried-up salt lakes and desert.

Generally, the hot summer sun is moderated along the coast by a steady breeze coming in from the sea. In fact, this cooling wind creates a sun-bathing hazard for newcomers, who overdo the toasting in the first day or two. The breeze gives a false sense of security that the sun's 'not really' so intense. Be warned!

Occasionally the wind changes direction, with dramatic effect. Instead of the breeze coming in from the sea, it arrives super-heated from the Sahara. Within minutes, the temperature can rocket, like switching on a hot-air blower. Suddenly it can reach 100 degrees Fahrenheit and you're experiencing the famous sirocco, curse of the Foreign Legion!

Temperatures and prices are at their highest in the July-August peak season, and sightseeing is sweltering. You can probably maximize enjoyment of Tunisia by avoiding the high season and choosing months when you can combine more ambitious sightseeing with your guaranteed suntan.

Most hotel tariffs operate in three bands: low season, November to February inclusive; middle season, March till the end of June, and in

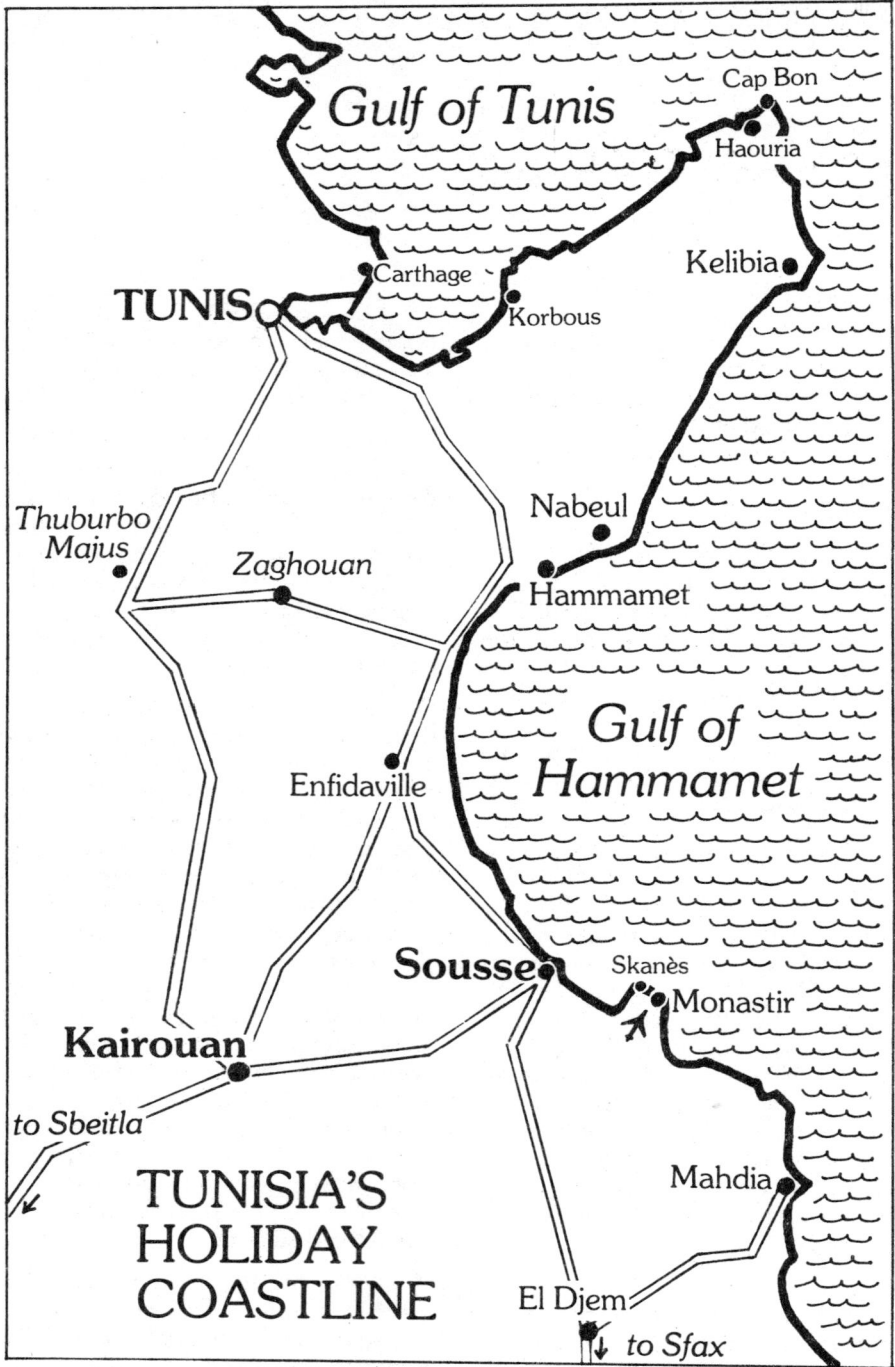

Gulf of Tunis

Cap Bon
Haouria

Kelibia

Carthage

TUNIS

Korbous

Nabeul

Thuburbo
Majus

Zaghouan

Hammamet

Gulf of
Hammamet

Enfidaville

Sousse

Skanès
Monastir

Kairouan

to Sbeitla

TUNISIA'S
HOLIDAY
COASTLINE

Mahdia

El Djem
to Sfax

September-October; high season, July-August. Tariffs are displayed in all rooms, and stamped by the local tourist office. The bulk of the business is from Easter till late October, but a 'winter' holiday is well worth considering - particularly if you want to explore the Saharan south or the great archaeological sites.

Which Airport?

The number one airport for handling charter-flight holiday traffic is Monastir. Its location, at the southern curved end of the Gulf of Hammamet, is ideal. You're right there for the resort hotels of Skanès and Monastir; only a short drive to the hotel strip that runs from the centre of Sousse to Port El Kantaoui; or a 90-minute drive to Hammamet, and thence to Nabeul. There's even an airport railway station, just outside the car park, with frequent services into Sousse or Monastir.

Tunis Carthage airport lies north of the capital, and is mainly geared to scheduled-service flights, with Tunis Air operating direct from Heathrow, and GB Airways from Gatwick. It's handiest for business traffic into Tunis, or for holiday visitors to the coastline around Sidi Bou Said. But transfers to Hammamet or Nabeul take a bit longer than from Monastir.

Serving the southern resorts are the airports of Sfax (most convenient if you're staying on the Kerkennah Islands) and Djerba (on the northern tip of the island, within easy drive of the holiday coastline past the capital, Houmt Souk).

On departure, don't forget to spend or exchange your final leftover dinars, which are useless outside Tunisia. Monastir airport, for instance, is well equipped to help you make final souvenir purchases. Also on sale are posies of jasmine buds, to show someone back home that you remembered them. Don't buy young palm-trees with soil and roots dangling, as their entry into Britain is forbidden. The French have no such ban, which explains why the palms are on sale.

Duty-frees, payable only in non-Tunisian hard currency, are available at the standard airport prices. If you enjoyed Thibarine liqueur during your holiday in Tunisia, the duty-free export price is £4.30.

If you have bought a very large cuddly camel or a bird-cage, have these items checked. Few aircraft can seat woolly camels and still have room for passengers. Flying with a large bird-cage on your lap is strictly for the birds.

Accommodation

Having come latish onto the tourism scene, Tunisia has taken warning from the Costa del Concreto development of other Mediterranean countries. With very few exceptions, Tunisia has steered clear of the international anonymous high-rise shoe-box design of glass and concrete. Instead, most hotels are tastefully planned in Moorish or Andalusian style, nothing higher than a palm tree, and surrounded by luxuriant gardens.

Resort hotels are grouped mainly in Hammamet/Nabeul, North Sousse/Port El Kantaoui, Skanès/Monastir and on the north-east coast of Djerba. In each of these areas, the pattern is similar. Hotels are spread out, very low density, for several miles along the beaches. Virtually every hotel has its own wide shoreline frontage, with in-depth grounds. The larger hotels operate like self-contained resorts, with all sport, leisure, shopping and entertainment facilities within the complex. A round-the-clock gatekeeper excludes any unwanted visitors.

In most of the tourist zones, hotels are served by a Route Touristique which runs parallel to the coastline, used only by light local traffic. Visitors who go wobbling around on hired bikes can feel reasonably safe, especially if they remember to keep to the right.

Getting more contact with Tunisia may entail a bus or taxi ride, though some hotels operate a free shuttle minibus service to the resort centre, which may be several miles away. If you like to potter regularly around the town shops and sights, better pick a hotel within strolling distance. Holiday brochures usually give a clear idea on location.

Tunisia follows the standard international system of hotel classification from one to four stars, topped by 4-star de luxe. You can reckon that all 4-star hotels will have total air conditioning; 3-star hotels in public rooms only. Swimming pools are standard in all 3- and 4-star resort hotels, and even in some 2-star.

Three-star hotels account for most of the package-holiday traffic from Britain, with 4-star and 4-star de luxe choice for those who can afford the higher standards of comfort and service. In some hotels, accommodation is spread around the grounds in bungalows, dripping with bougainvillaea or nestling in the shade of palm-trees. You can mix privacy with your hotel life-style. At a typical luxury establishment, each room has its individual walled terrace, so that sun-worshippers can get an all-over

tan, with no white patches anywhere. Study the brochure photos and write-ups for an idea of the layout.

The very largest of the hotels operate like self-contained holiday centres. A typical establishment, with capacity of around 2000 beds, is an extensive development stretching along several hundred yards of powder-fine beach, equipped with sunloungers and a forest of thatched umbrellas. The complex looks like a small town, based on low-rise blocks of bedrooms.

Everything focuses on a central courtyard, constantly bustling with travel agency rep offices, souvenir stores, news-stand, cafés and restaurants of different grades. In another central area, local musicians entertain. Happy snaps are displayed of the events of the previous day or two. As part of the entertainment facilities, four film shows rotate every evening, in different languages, with free entrance.

For sport-lovers there are ping-pong tables, notices of competitive events, programmes of 'animation', gymnastics, volleyball, water polo, aerobics. Tennis, sailing and windsurfing are all free in low season.

Photographic angles abound, with pools, archways and flowers galore. A whole narrow street reproduces the atmosphere of a Tunisian souk, with craft and souvenir stores of all types. There's really no need to emerge from the hotel grounds during the whole stay, except for excursions to look at Tunisia from the air-conditioned comfort of a motor coach.

At the other extreme, offering minimum facilities, 2-star hotels are great value for budget-watchers who accept simple accommodation and unpretentious public rooms. But don't expect too much from a modest 2-star hotel! The price-ticket is a fabulous bargain in terms of flight, transfers, services of local rep, and basic accommodation. But two stars is two stars, and one cannot expect 4-star luxury.

However, if you just want somewhere to sleep, perhaps intending to spend much of your time exploring the country, then 2 stars can be adequate. These simpler hotels are mostly located near town centres, handier to transport rather than beaches. It's still possible to use the facilities of higher-grade hotels, who may charge a dinar or two for access to their pool. They also welcome the extra bar and lunch business.

Service

Tunisia has a long tradition of sheep-herding and agriculture, but is a relative newcomer to the service industries. Growth of tourism has outpaced the training facilities in catering schools, and many employees in hotels and restaurants have picked up their skills on the job.

Young waiters - first generation out of the villages - may not yet have qualifications for the Hilton, but they are cheerful and willing. Their French is usually more fluent than that of most hotel guests, but their English, German or Swedish may be somewhat more fractured. They compensate by smiling a lot.

Life in a warm country like Tunisia is lived at a somewhat leisurely pace. It's no use getting furious because service doesn't respond instantly at the snap of a finger. Part of the holiday is to relax into the south-Mediterranean rhythm, and you'll have no compaints about service.

Hotel Food

Most holiday-hotel menus are 'international' - aimed to please the majority of the mainly French, German and British clientele. Tunisia is not one of the world's great gourmet destinations, but standards of cuisine are good, thanks to a well-established heritage from the French occupation.

Hotel menus usually include a sprinkling of more typical Tunisian specialties. If you like to dine out from time to time, or take whole-day sightseeing trips, it's best to book a half-board package. Half board usually means an evening meal, but many hotels are cooperative about swapping lunch for dinner, especially if you give advance notice. Hotel lunches are frequently served buffet style near the pool.

Tunisian hotel breakfasts are basic Continental: French bread, butter, pre-boiled egg, marmalade, prickly-pear or quince jam, tea or coffee. Anything cooked to order will be 'extra'.

Catering for Children

The normal package-holiday deal is that infants under two years of age on the day of holiday departure travel free on an adult's lap. Sometimes there's a modest charge to cover airport taxes. At the chosen hotel, cot hire and cost of food are then payable direct.

From the age of two, children usually qualify for a tour-operator discount unless they occupy a separate room. Reductions vary greatly according to time of season. Early May, child discount could be 35% or even 50% for a youngster sharing a room with two adults; but only half those levels in the high-season weeks of July-August.

A few hotels have four-berth family rooms, so that two children can each get the discount. Sometimes - particularly off-season - single-parent families are offered special deals. Likewise, some operators feature low-season offers of 'three weeks for the price of two', or single rooms without supplement. Check details in the holiday-brochure conditions.

In fact, Tunsisia's mid-summer months can be over-hot for youngsters - just like anywhere else in the Mediterranean. May or October are preferable, besides being much cheaper.

A major safety factor is that many hotels have grounds and gardens that flow straight onto the beach, and are not separated by a busy highway. Resort beaches are perfect for the bucket-and-spade clientele, with beautiful soft sand that gently shelves into a shallow sea. Often the kids can wade 20 yards out, before getting their bottoms wet.

Even in high season, the uncrowded beaches linked to the resort hotels offer more than ample elbow-room for castle-building projects. Larger hotels cater specially for children, with paddling pool, playroom and playground, kiddies' 'club' with supervisor, early suppers and baby-sitting or baby patrol service. Depending on the hotel, or the tour operator, club programmes can include beach games, hiking, swimming galas and Fancy Dress events.

Often it's feasible to leave offspring in good hands, while parents embark on sightseeing trips. Trips to archaeological sites aren't much fun for younger children. Safaris to the South - Matmata cave-dwellers, and the oases - are much more of a thrill,

though road distances can be tiring.

For evening entertainment, the standard 'Bedouin Feast' and similar outings are quite suitable for children, who enjoy the joyous circus atmosphere of horse-riding, juggling and acrobatics. Indeed, these tourist events are deliberately operated early evening so as to encourage family attendance.

The Beaches

Superb beaches of fine white or golden sands are reason enough for choosing Tunisia. Most of the developed beaches are tended by individual hotels, with a commercial interest in ensuring that their patch is kept clean. The majority are spotless. Any litter-strewn beaches are usually closer to resort centres, more accessible to the general public, and are nobody's baby except the municipality's.

Hotels set out a tempting array of loungers and thatched parasols on 'their' sands, with waiters around to serve cool drinks and snacks. Although beaches are public, they still feel private, particularly at hotels which are a mile or two out of town. Hotel staff can usually discourage noisier teenagers from disturbing guests who want to siesta in peace.

Even so, many holidaymakers prefer to stay around the pool. An advantage is that you can dodge the stream of beach vendors, eager to sell carpets or woolly camels. Likewise, the more decorative topless guests can concentrate on their suntan without being embarrassed by Tunisian youths who want to prove their virility.

For Garden-lovers

Much pleasure in staying at well-established resort hotels comes from their luxuriant gardens: green with shade, alternating with vibrant colours of tropical flowers, all attracting plentiful birdlife and bird-song. Because labour costs are low, hotels can afford to run a substantial work-force, to keep everything neat and well-watered.

Part of the interest comes from watching gardeners at work. A gardener will pull out a weed or two, water the ground which has been vacated, and then patiently wait - maybe with a little Arabic song to pass the time - until the next weed appears. It hardly looks like high pressure, but the end result is an Arabian Nights' dream heavy with the scent of jasmine.

If you want that style of garden setting, avoid the spanking-new hotels, unmasked in the brochures as an artist's impression rather than a photograph. The first wave of guests may enjoy watching the concrete dry, but an instant garden is more difficult. Hopeful palm-trees and shrubs planted in the scorched earth won't provide a shady environment for at least five years. The hotel complex will be bare of foliage, green lawns and the chirrup of birdlife.

Self-Catering

For maximum independence, many holidaymakers prefer self-catering. In Tunisia the choice of apartments is very limited - nothing like the massive volume available in other Med destinations like Spain or Malta. Some tour operators offer package holidays based on the few purpose-built apartment or villa complexes in the principal resorts.

In general, Tunisia lacks the large reservoir of privately-owned holiday accommodation which is the basis of self-catering business in other countries. However, particularly out of high season, an independent-minded flight-only traveller could arrive without advance booking and find something suitable through on-the-spot agencies.

Shopping for food supplies is no problem. The purpose-built developments normally include a handy food store; or you can shop in the resort centre at self-service groceries and supermarkets where prices will probably be lower. More fun, you can go ethnic and shop for your fruit, vegetables and groceries in the souks - though buying meat supplies in the medina may suddenly convert you to vegetarianism. Butcher's shops are usually painted pink, and often have a grisly habit of hanging out a cow's head or a sheep's head to prove they are selling fresh meat and it's not donkey or camel.

Youth Travel

Tunisia's Youth Hostel Association is a member of the International Federation, so that a YHA card is accepted. Bed-night price is around one dinar at the two dozen hostels spread around the main holiday destinations.

Hostels are located at Ain Draham, Beja, Bizerta, La Chebba, Gabès, Gafsa, Djerba, Kairouan, Kasserine, Kelibia, Le Kef, Médenine, Menzel Temime, Monastir, Nabeul, Seliana, Sfax, Sidi Bouzid, Sousse, Tozeur, Tunis, Zaghouan and Zarzis.

Camping is not permitted at hostels, except at Nabeul. Elsewhere it's permissible to pitch a tent on a beach or in a park, after getting authorization from the nearest Police or National Guard Station, or from the property owner.

Flight only

Some of Tunisia's best travel bargains are in the 'seat-only' sector of holiday business. Quite simply, when a tour operator assembles a package of accommodation linked with charter flight, he hopes all the contracted holidays will be sold before the aircraft takes off. Otherwise he loses money, through aircraft seats that fly empty. Hence the solution of offering flight-only tickets that cost much less than the regular scheduled-service fares.

Recognising this growing trend towards flight-only sales, leading operators bring order into the somewhat chaotic business by publishing flight-only brochures under a variety of brand-names. Instead of waiting for last-minute availability, holidaymakers can book ahead for the flight and date they want. These flights are often more convenient than the scheduled services out of London Heathrow. Thus, Britannia Airways offer numerous departures to Monastir every week year-round, from Gatwick, Luton, Bristol, Birmingham, East Midlands, Manchester and Glasgow.

Typical travellers are adventure-minded and young, without family commitments - split between backpackers and young professionals. Often it's just the low price which triggers the impulse decision to travel.

The backpackers are confident enough to find their own accommodation on arrival, in some of Tunisia's more modest hotels and youth hostels. In high season, the seat-only traveller may have problems in finding a room. The Tunisian National Tourist Office in London can supply a free hotel guide. If no advance arrangements have been made, the first few days could be a headache. But outside the July-August peak, accommodation can usually be found. Local tourist offices can recommend a vacancy in your price range.

During low season, there's really no accommodation problem. The flight-only deal can then be ideal for travellers who want to move around Tunisia, exploring the country, rather than staying in one place.

Sport and Water Activities

Virtually every hotel can offer a standard range of filtered swimming pool with background music, sun terraces, bars and barbecues. Likewise, there's good choice of the more active water-sports: sailing-boats, pedaloes, water-skiing, parascending and the like. Many people enjoy being in the water with a windsurfer. Standing up is another problem, and the larger hotels usually have someone on the staff who gives instruction. Scuba-diver enthusiasts should investigate the potential of the Tabarka area, where coral is the principal underwater attraction.

For terra firma activities, hotels feature a variety of sport facilities, from shuffleboard to tennis and ping-pong, mini-golf, bicycle and moped hire. If golf is your scene, choose Sousse-Nord or Port El Kantaoui, where 27 holes are well established, with another 9 holes to come.

Horse and Camel Riding

Most holidaymakers who go horse-riding know what to expect, but camels are different. However hard

20

you try to dodge, at some stage in a Tunisian holiday you'll probably be persuaded against your better judgement into boarding a camel, the infamous ship of the desert which makes you feel seasick.

For camel and horse rides alike, always agree your price before mounting. If you disagree when you're up in the saddle, it may be easy enough to leap off a horse. But have you ever tried getting off a camel when it's standing up? Price for an hour is something like 5 dinars, depending on how the bargaining goes. You are expected to pay the owner, not vice versa.

Be prepared for a rough take-off with no seat-belts provided. Clutch tight in readiness for three mighty jerks as the animal rises from the knees-bend position into its full towering height. Then off you go, with camel and his owner in full command.

Thankfully, all things come to an end, even purgatory. Your camel will make a three-point landing: first to kneel at the front end; then down with the back end; finally level out, to permit you to topple off, overjoyed at survival.

The objective of the ordeal is to have your photograph taken, preferably dressed in authentic costume like a Sheikh of Araby. You can boast about it for years after - 'The time I rode out into the desert (or across a neighbouring hotel building site) aboard the most uncomfortable camel in the Sahara. . .' The full dramatic details can be expanded, to taste. Nobody ever really enjoys a camel ride, but it's all part of the Tunisian experience. Clued-up travellers cut the torture down to one dinar for five minutes - enough time for a ground-based photographer to take those obligatory pictures for posterity.

Night-Life

Compared with other Mediterranean destinations, Tunisia is light on nightlife. In all the beach resorts, the decibel count is low. There are no focal-point areas thick with discos, all running at full volume. Likewise, you don't get lines of crowded bars in Spanish style where you rub shoulders with the locals. As a Moslem country, Tunisia lacks the hard-drinking tradition of Spain, France, Italy, Greece or Yugoslavia. The majority of Tunisians are teetotal, hooked on mint tea, and they don't drink alcohol very visibly in public.

Most resorts have a cinema where varied-language films are shown, while hotels themselves usually offer a programme of videos. TV is not very rewarding, unless your Arabic or French is fluent. More hotels are being equipped with dish aerials that receive other European-language programmes.

Each major hotel offers its own in-house entertainment, which is unlikely to go through the roof. Apart from the inevitable 'night-club' with maybe a three-piece Tunisian band, a quiet after-dinner drink around the pool is about the wildest it gets. Some hotels play records in the bar and call it a disco.

Maybe once or twice a week, a folk-lore group will arrive and bang drums, rattle cymbals, blow pipes and balance earthenware pots on their heads. They dance in local costumes, and lure visitors to join in. If a belly-dancer is included, the success of audience participation is assured. Excited husbands seize the opportunity to drape their arms round a belly-dancer while wifey takes a picture.

21

To extend the range of after-dinner entertainment, you can go on a hotel-crawl. Local travel-agency reps can advise where the action is, from night to night - dancing, discos, folklore shows and the like.

Some hotels - particularly those favoured by the French - employ 'animators'. They're rather like Butlin's Redcoats, who organise you into funny games, competitions, sports, tournaments and the like. The animators are full of jolly japes like tossing guests into the pool, or giving theatre shows in drag. But, if all this is not your glass of tea, you can easily stay aloof.

One thing you shouldn't miss: a 'Bedouin Feast' or similar folklore show. It's good-value tourist entertainment, usually with transport, evening meal of Tunisian specialities, and freely-flowing wine included in the price. At a typical show, some 600 guests are seated at tables around a circus-type arena, giving everyone a good view.

There are professional acrobats, jugglers, fire-eaters and sword-swallowers, with pulsating Tunisian folk music and dance. It's the tourist equivalent of the entertainers who traditionally perform in North African cities towards sunset: acrobats, drummers, wind musicians, snake charmers, story-tellers and the like. Waiters join in the fun, acting as cheer-leaders and balancing platters of food or bottles of wine on their heads. Highlight of the show is a thrilling display of Arab horsemanship in the fantasia tradition. Splendid stallions dance to the pounding rhythm of Bedouin pipes and an enormous drum called a *tabla*.

These shows mostly start early, about 6 p.m., and are often finished by 9.30 or 10 p.m. - quite suitable family entertainment. Even the belly-dancers would not cause grandma to blush.

FESTIVALS

Summer is the season of festivals. Annually, Tunisia holds around 250 festivals on a national, regional or local level. On arrival at your holiday hotel, check what's on offer in the region. It's worth making a special effort to attend one of these events. Here's a sample listing, with approximate dates (which change from year to year).

Carthage - July-August - a classic festival held at the site of the ancient Roman theatre, with international stars from East and West.

Hammamet - all July until mid-August - held at the Hammamet Cultural Centre in a 1,000-seat circular Greek-style theatre, this is an avant-garde event which actively promotes new Tunisian talent in music, theatre and dance.

Tabarka - July-August - when culture takes over in a small fishing village of 5000 inhabitants, amid a setting of a deserted beach backed by pine trees. Musicians, painters, singers and artistes mingle informally with holidaymakers.

Monastir - July - similar to the Festival of Carthage, with local caricature and comic entertainment shows.

Dougga - July - a theatre festival of national and foreign plays, held in the splendid Roman theatre.

Sousse - all July until mid-August - festival of puppets, processions, variety shows and local folklore.

Douz - late December - a Saharan festival devoted to the cultural riches of the South: folklore, camel racing, Bedouin crafts, sand-skiing etc.

Testour - Malouf and Arab Music - June - festival of traditional Arabic music of Andalusian origin.

Sightseeing

Even the most dedicated sun-worshipper will expect to take time off for sightseeing. Each of the principal cities has something different to offer. All have an Arab-style walled inner town - the medina, with trading souks and a central Friday mosque. Schedule a visit for the bring-and-buy market day, when country folk arrive with fruit, vegetables and a sheep or two, and do their own weekly shopping with the proceeds.

The handiest markets for the main holiday resorts are Nabeul on Fridays, Sousse on Sundays, and Midoun in the island of Djerba on Fridays. (Other market days are listed in Chapter 12 on Shopping.) All these markets provide splendid photo subjects, with colourful scenes everywhere you point the camera. Travel-agency coach excursions save you travelling on very crowded local buses, which are cheaper but very ethnic. Sunday excursions to Sousse also include folk-music and flag-waving at the kasbah museum, a visit to the Grand Mosque, a walk on the city ramparts and a tour of the medina.

Excursions to Tunis - medina and Bardo Museum, Carthage and Sidi Bou Said - are most easily arranged from the Hammamet-Nabeul area. Once you have the layout, it's easy to travel individually by rail or road into the capital for extra shopping and sightseeing. Distances are greater from the Monastir and Sousse area, but Tunis still makes an easy day trip.

Inland, the main excursion targets are the Roman remains at El Djem, Dougga, Zaghouan, Thurburbo Majus and the rest. Not-to-be-missed is a half-day swing to Kairouan, Islam's fourth holiest city with historic mosques, fascinating souks, and superb displays of hand-made carpets.

Most memorable of all, you can go by air-conditioned coach or minibus to the desert south, land of oases and cavemen. There is good choice of one-day to three-day safaris, with meals and accommodation included.

All these excursions are tried-and-tested itineraries which operate smoothly with qualified guides. Prices are very little different from what an experienced traveller would pay on a go-it-alone basis. By the time you have used public transport, with a cab each way to the bus or louage station, entrance fees and the like, then you may have saved yourself a dinar or two. But it's hardly worth the sweat, particularly as there is a substantial distance between each of the main sites. For the average visitor, it's certainly not worth the effort of trying to do the sightseeing cheaper. But a really independent character may prefer to rent a self-drive car.

The majority of the tour coaches are air-conditioned, mostly Mercedes-Benz or Swedish Volvo, comfortable with reclining seats and good PA systems. Many of the tours start early, to pack the maximum possible interest into the day, and to get the bulk of travel and sightseeing done before the sun is running at full strength. At the average 7.30 departure time, little groups of holidaymakers wait at hotel entrances for their excursion coaches to arrive. The first half-hour can go on the pick-up circuit. But, for a garden-lover, that can provide bonus enjoyment, to admire the flower displays in each hotel's grounds.

Desert Safaris

Coach or minibus excursions from holiday resorts to the oases of Southern Tunisia offer a good taster of desert sightseeing while keeping to the tarred highways. But there's a more ambitious style of adventure-packed odyssey based on Land Rovers and trucks purpose-built with special tyres for riding the sand-dunes. Safaris are operated along the desert trails of southern Tunisia, staying overnight in tents. Guides and drivers are highly experienced at this brand of tourism.

During the cooler winter months from November onwards, a few expeditions even travel across the desert to West Africa and the Cameroons. The flat rooves of the vehicles are equipped for viewing wildlife in the game-rich areas of Africa further south. Tunisia can be the launching-pad for the trip of a lifetime!

D.I.Y. Travel

With most of Tunisia's resorts spread along several miles of coastline, some hotels offer minibus transport into the town centre. In addition, there are regular bus services. A snag: if you're staying part-way along the Route Touristique, at popular times the bus will already be full with passengers from previous hotel-stops.

Between Hammamet and Nabeul, and between Monastir, Skanès and Sousse, a suburban-type train clatters along, parallel to the coast. If there's a halt near your hotel, it's worth making careful note of scheduled times throughout the day. Between Sousse and Port El Kantaoui, a highly popular blue Noddy train trundles along the

coast road, often with every seat taken from the start.

Fortunately, taxis are reasonably priced, only about 10p on flag-down. They are very handy for shorter journeys. Beat-up four-seater Peugeot cabs cruise around the hotel entrances, so it's not usually necessary to telephone specially. They have a licence number on the roof, along with a taxi sign and a meter inside. If the driver forgets to switch on the meter, remind him. Pay what's on the meter, plus a small tip. After 9 p.m., there's 50% surcharge. The addition is done by mental arithmetic, rather than by meter. Watch out for the larger taxis, like estate cars and Mercedes. Their meters go round twice as fast.

If you want to explore Tunisia on your own, supplementing the travel-agency excursions, there is good choice of public road and rail transport between the main cities. But if you're aiming to visit more remote archaeological sites, away in open country, then the logistics become more complicated, making car hire or coach tour more preferable.

Inter-city buses are low-cost, but are often crowded and can be somewhat grotty. Services are usually frequent in early morning, but fade by evening time. Be sure to check return schedules.

A useful alternative is the louage system of shared taxis which operate along set routes. Mostly they are six-seater Peugeot estate cars, somewhat elderly and battered from shuttling back and forth, fully loaded. You pay a single-seat tariff, which is very little more than a bus fare.

In each town centre there's a recognised louage departure point - a scene of some confusion in the principal cities - with vehicles lined up for take-off to their varied destinations. Some of the vehicles have a destination label on the windscreen, but check anyway. When all five passenger seats are filled, off you whirl. Overloading is not permitted. Sometimes, when customers are scarce, the driver will depart with several seats vacant, hoping to pick up fares en route. If you speak reasonable French, you can have an amusing time, with driver and the other passengers eager to talk. Don't expect anyone to speak English!

Rail services are useful, up and down the coast. The main line from Tunis serves Bir Bou Rekba (the junction for Hammamet and Nabeul), Sousse, El Djem (for the Roman Colosseum) and thence to Sfax and Gabès. Check timings carefully, as services are somewhat infrequent. Missing a train can mean waiting several hours for the next. From Sfax there's a once-daily service to the oasis of Gafsa, and thence Metlaoui (junction for the highly scenic train-buff journey up the Seldja Gorge) and Tozeur.

First class on the longer-distance Tunisian trains is quite comfortable, with reclining seats. Some carriages have air conditioning, for which you pay a little extra. Even second class offers tolerable comfort, but the seats are harder, with less leg-room. The price gap between 1st and 2nd class is relatively small, so you might as well travel in style, unless your budget is very tight.

Car hire

If you prefer hiring a self-drive car, remember that Tunisia has one of the world's highest accident rates when related to the number of vehicles on the road. Efforts are being made to encourage people to belt up. But, till now, the advantages of seat belts do not seem to have persuaded the local drivers. It's also part of the local macho image to jump red lights. Sometimes you see kids, not even teenage, riding light motor bikes in slap-happy style, no helmets. There's no minimum age limit for riding lower-powered bikes. Maybe it's a substitute for birth control.

So be prepared for wild happenings, especially from jay-walkers, lane-switchers and cowboy tactics generally. Also, in a country where rain comes seldom, be ready for skiddy roads after a light rain.

Tunisia must be one of the world's few countries where you rarely see a Japanese car. Cars are mostly of French design, assembled in Tunisian assembly plants. Traffic is mainly Renaults, Peugeots and donkey-carts, with some Mercedes. Reckon about £30 a day for car hire, by the time you add mileage and the cost of petrol.

For more local use, it's easy to hire small motor-bikes, costing about £10 for half day, or £13 for full day. They can take a pillion passenger. Also available are push-bikes: half-day about £2; whole day £3.

Road signs are in French style, with translations into Arabic.

3. The Beaches of Cap Bon

Hammamet

Mileage from Hammamet: Tunis 40; Sousse 50; Sfax 130; Gabès 215; Gafsa 195; Tozeur 250; Djerba 320.

Hammamet, together with adjoining Nabeul, ranks as the prime garden-resort of North Africa, with fine beaches of soft sand. Prewar, this charming haven was discovered by a wealthy international set of artists, writers and beautiful people who built elegant villas amid perfumed gardens and citrus groves. Of course, the Romans were there first, leaving a few remains, and Hammamet centres upon a kasbah and walled medina that dates from 15th century. But Hammamet's greatest development has come in the past 30 years, thanks to building of hotels for a year-round season of charter-flight holidaymaking. In 1950, when the present author stayed in Hammamet, the sleepy little fishing village had precisely one hotel of any calibre.

Today's complexes are well spaced along several miles of coast, each side of the headland - Hammamet-Sud and Hammamet-Nord, which continues into Nabeul, where tariffs are a shade lower. Nothing obtrudes. It's hard to believe that here is Tunisia's largest concentration of holiday accommodation, with capacity of 30,000 beds. White bungalows and pavilions are set amid green foliage, and no building is higher than a palm tree. There are seven four-star establishments, of which two are luxury-grade, and about thirty three-star. None of them fouls the waterfront with multi-storeyed concrete.

Maybe, in years to come, all the intervening spaces will be developed. Meanwhile, through the 1990's, this air of spaciousness is unlikely to change. The superb golden beach compares favourably with almost anywhere in the world.

Following a standard Tunisian pattern, a Route Touristique serves the main hotels and holiday villages, whose gardens open direct onto the sands. During the day, the easiest way to visit neighbouring hotels is just to stroll along the beach. The regular main road - hot and dusty - runs parallel, but further inland.

The Kasbah

Hollywood would take kindly to the Kasbah, which was a Foreign Legion garrison during French-occupation days. It has been restored with rebuilt ramparts and a Moorish café on the top, and is open daily from 9.00 till 20.00 hrs. Built in its present square format in 1474, on the site of a 12th-century fortress, the Kasbah looks like a purpose-built stage set. The 35p entrance fee is good value. Ancient cannons are set around the inner courtyard, which also features the domed shrine of Sidi Bou-Ali, a 14th-century holy man who rests in a green and red coffin. Sometimes the courtyard is setting for cultural and folklore shows.

The Kasbah ramparts give the best all-embracing view of the sweeping bay, with brightly painted fishing boats drawn up on the beach or floating just off-shore. All around is a bird's-eye view of rooftop Hammamet. Every medina house is brilliantly colour-washed. Terraced rooves have sitting areas marked by decorative glazed tiles that sparkle in the sunshine. It's a good place to catch a breeze, judging from the shirts and underwear which flap on rooftop washing lines among the tall TV aerials that can get Italy. Take your camera for photographs, including stunning sunsets. For added sound effects, listen to the evocative clamour of muezzin loudspeakers from a dozen mosques, calling the faithful to prayer. The chorus continues at least five minutes, with some muezzins starting their call as others are finishing.

The Kasbah also houses something off-beat: the International Museum of the Ram - '. . . devoted to the history of this prodigious animal in ancient civilizations, religions and mythologies. From time immemorial, the ram was invested with a divine character - worshipped, and regarded with respect, admiration and even fear, because of the power and influence it was thought to hold over men and events.

'The exhibits and pictures displayed in this museum convey the thoughts, messages and dreams of past generations of the human race. The purpose in creating this museum is to bring back to man's memory the past glory of this sacred animal, which was and still is man's companion and an eye-witness of his civilization through history.'

Probably the animals did not feel too happy with some aspects of man's civilization. Many of the sculptures depict rams being sacrificed in order to please the gods.

The Medina

The walled Medina follows the traditional structure of an Arab town, which places high value on family privacy. The nucleus of an Arab house is the very private inner courtyard, contrasting with the Greek or Italian style, where the front doorstep is part of the living space, in public view.

Likewise, this shows in a separation between commercial areas and residential. Maybe the distinction is rather less in modern Hammamet, where craft workshops have spread into residential areas, and every passing visitor is yanked inside. Buildings just inside the Medina entrance gates have switched entirely to souvenir business.

But a stroll through the Medina offers visual delight, along well-swept lanes with contented cats' basking on whitewashed cobbles. Houses have beautiful grillwork windows and solid wooden doors with tiled surrounds, or carved stonework porches from Dar Chaabane, the stone-mason's village near Nabeul. You get glimpses of tiled courtyards within.

Signs point either to the Maison Arabe or to the Brothers' Shop 'where you will be surprised by the prices and the quality'. One of the brothers is a local teacher of English, who formerly taught 6th-form French at Leicester. Turning down by The Brothers' shop brings you out onto the fortress walls, where local lads fish from the rocks.

Getting lost in the medina doesn't really matter, as the maze is relatively small. Sooner or later, you emerge again by the city wall or onto the beach, and can then easily zero back to your starting point.

The Commercial Centre

Just across the highway from the Kasbah is the modern Commercial Centre - a pedestrian precinct with Tunisian banks, snack bars, terrace restaurants, boutiques and carpet stores. It's all tightly clustered at the bottom end of Avenue Bourguiba, which is the nearest approach to a traditional seaside promenade, complete with Tourist Information Centre.

Inner focal-point for the Commercial Centre is a camel-powered well, which looks Heath Robinson but works splendidly. The resident camel journeys round in a dizzy circle, to operate a revolving rope ladder, with an amphora-shaped earthenware jar lashed to each rung. Water is scooped up, rises, is tipped out, and then circles down empty again for a refill.

At the supermarket called Magasin Générale self-caterers can buy alcohol supplies. Opposite side to the Post Office, on Avenue de la République, maybe you can find yesterday's English newspapers. Wednesday evening and Thursday morning there's a local produce market of fruit and vegetables, on the town outskirts along the road towards Nabeul.

Municipal Museum

Next to the PTT - Post Office - is a small town museum, ethnic: several rooms with plaster bodies and faces to display traditional costume. But this is no Madame Tussaud's. The figures all look as though they have experienced some ultimate horror, including one poor soul who is working a grindstone.

There are also the standard glass cases of ancient weapons, jewelry, pottery and glass. A coin collection illustrates the history of Tunisia through its pocket money, with finds from Carthaginian times, Roman, Vandal, Byzantine, Fatimides, Almohades, and so on through to coinage introduced by the French. The museum is worth the 20p entrance, and ten minutes of your holiday.

International Cultural Centre

Described by American architect Frank Lloyd Wright as 'the most beautiful house I know,' the residence of the prewar Romanian millionaire, Georges Sebastian, is now Hammamet's Cultural Centre. The magnificent 22-acre garden is paradise in springtime, with the scent of flowers and chirrup of birdlife, including hoopoes, goldfinches and bee eaters. From the villa terrace is a superb view over trees and cactus, to the beach where horses gallop.

An annual festival of music, theatre and dance runs throughout July and half of August. The Gulbenkian Foundation contributed to the 1964 construction of an open-air theatre in the garden. Built in simple Greek style with circular stage, it seats a thousand.

Georges Sebastian's house itself is pure fantasy, and includes a swimming pool completely walled and floored with marble slabs. Furnishings are simple, like a refectory table, 15 feet long, which is a solid block of black marble. Among the distinguished prewar guests were Elsa Schiaparelli of Shocking Pink perfume fame, André Gide and Paul Klee. During wartime days, Rommel, Montgomery, King George V1, Churchill and Eisenhower all lodged here, though not simultaneously. Don't miss it!

NABEUL

The market centre of Nabeul sleeps six days a week, and then bubbles over every Friday for its 'camel market'. Here's a slight misunderstanding. Many visitors expect to see hundreds of live camels, being bought and sold after lengthy haggling. Reality is somewhat different. But then who expects a Parisian flea market to be jumping?

Yet, in fact, there's an enormous number of camels for sale! As you enter the main street towards the market area, every shop is festooned with hundreds of woolly camels: big, little and middling. On the pavements outside are long caravan lines of olive-wood dromedaries. Pottery shops have camels stacked on every shelf, and brassware stores are onto the same bandwagon.

As visitors surge forward, there are camels to right of them, camels to left of them, camels in front of them. Their's but to look and buy. Most succumb. It develops into a kind of buying fever, as visitors keep remembering yet another child back home who would just love a camel to cuddle. At a random guestimate, each visitor finally buys an average of 2.7 camels, and local tour buses are designed to hold 40 passengers, 108 dromedaries, 23 carpets and 97 miscellaneous items of pottery.

Nabeul is the prime craft centre of Tunisia, and Friday's market is the most important single sales outlet. But, despite the heavy accent on products for the holiday trade, all the local citizens are there, too, with their weekly shopping lists: fruit and veg, spices, nuts, grain, textiles and groceries. It's a lively, enjoyable occasion.

Entrance to the so-called Camel Market itself costs 20p. In the enclosed area, a fleet of some fifty ships of the desert await. It's a camel-ride market, where tourists can climb aboard and be led around the ring, five minutes' plain sailing for one dinar, while admiring companions take photos.

A bar serves drinks, but nothing alcoholic like a slug of brandy to steady the nerves after a camel-ride: just Boga, Fanta or Coke. Steps go to a terrace for a grandstand view of the show, which includes a display of Arab horsemanship. The terrace also overlooks a large open space where vendors display their craftware - pottery, sandals, carpets, blankets, copperware and of course a few more thousand cuddly woolly camels. Pictures galore!

Afterwards, go through a small gate in the wall for the 'real' Marché aux Chameaux, where sheep and goats are sold, and even a camel or two.

Ceramics

Nabeul is Tunisia's ceramic and tile capital. The choice of designs is vast, from stylized tradition to kitsch; from classical Greek to imitation Picasso. Production is split between everyday earthenware for household and garden, and the highly ornamented and glazed pieces intended for more decorative use. Visitors are welcomed in most workshops, where a master potter employs twenty or thirty assistants and apprentices on a small-scale production line. Most kilns have switched from olivewood-fired to electric, but otherwise the production methods are centuries' old. Men still roll out the clay, treading it with bare feet, adding water and folding it like pastry until the mud-bath is ripe for the wheel.

Traditional Nabeul colours are half-and-half yellow and green, made from ancient formulae: mixture of lead and antimony for yellow, or lead and copper oxide for green. European customers mainly prefer a combination of white with blue and turquoise, while Libyans go for brown or maroon. Big earthenware pots are exported to garden centres in France. Many Nabeul buildings gleam with glazed tiles. Ceramic panels with dazzling decorations are heavy to carry home, but worth the effort. Wrought iron is another local product where weight must be considered more than price.

At a central crossroads, a large traffic-island tree is surrounded by a huge decorated pot to publicize Nabeul's main industry. Look closer, and it's not pottery, but concrete.

Stone Carving

Just outside Nabeul is Dar Chaabane, a village of stone-masons. They specialise in making decorative porchways and carved columns for households and public buildings. The industry has flourished here since the 9th century AD. Symmetrical and geometric designs are stencilled on soft white limestone which chips like wood at the touch of a chisel. You constantly see the workmanship in the medinas of Hammamet or Tunis, while local houses are heavily embellished with samples.

As a sideline the workshops sell small ashtrays made from off-cuts - about the only item which a holidaymaker effectively can carry off as a souvenir.

Straw Products

Another craft specialty of the Nabeul area - in the town itself, or in the neighbouring village of Es Somaa - is the production of straw mats and rushwork baskets, cots and coasters. These products are sold by the craftsmen themselves in the Friday market; or through a cooperative sales outlet in the centre of Nabeul.

Blanket Weaving

Of social interest is the organization of a blanket-weaving cooperative, which began operating in 1962 at Beni Khiar - another small village near Nabeul. Weavers have shares in the co-op, but are not employees. Each makes his own hours, deciding for himself how often and how long to work at his own loom. Every member is paid immediately on a piece-work basis - so-much per square metre - and then shares in the overall profits at the year's end. Prices at the factory are very reasonable.

Perfume industry

Between Hammamet and Nabeul, great quantities of jasmine bushes are cultivated or grow wild. The scent is highly popular among the Arabs, who thread the flowers into necklaces. Street vendors sell posies of jasmine buds, or they are permitted by tolerant restaurant owners to offer their wares from table to table, so long as they don't pester. Arab youths often walk along smelling a bunch of jasmine, but it doesn't mean anything.

In Nabeul there's yet another industry: the distillation of perfume from plantations of oranges, roses and geraniums. Springtime, several local festivals are held. In Nabeul a March-April commercial fair is held, partly devoted to a Festival of Orange Blossom. Orange flower water is good for insomnia.

A few miles away across Cap Bon is Menzel Bou Zelfa, offering an Orange Tree Festival in the latter half of March: a regional event which shows the different types of orange, distillation of the blossom, and street entertainment. During the same period, a similar festival is held in the neighbouring township of Beni Khaled.

Local Transport

The centres of Nabeul and Hammamet are only seven miles apart, but their beaches extend the whole distance, spaced with hotel developments. A single-track railway runs parallel to the beach, with an infrequent service; but buses are every half hour. Fares are low, under 20p. If you're staying anywhere along the line, it's worth noting timetable details. Otherwise there are plentiful cabs. Shared-taxi 'louage' services do not operate between Hammamet and Nabeul. From most hotels you can rent a bike, horse or camel.

At Bir bou Rekba, a few miles west of Hammamet, the branch railway makes connection with main line trains to Tunis, or to Sousse and points south, with eight or nine daily trains each way. Likewise there are scheduled bus services into Tunis, costing about £1, mainly early morning and after lunch, with parallel times for the return journeys. Most visitors prefer to pay rather more for a travel-agency tour with door-to-door service.

Excursions

Hammamet and Nabeul are neatly placed for easy sightseeing, with good choice of coach tours. The most popular trip is a one-day swing to Tunis, visiting the souks and Bardo Museum, with a quick look at Carthage and a stroll through Sidi Bou Said. A half-day Tunis jaunt is billed as a shopping tour. Once you know the city layout, it's then quite simple to re-visit Tunis under your own steam, using public transport.

Packed with countryside interest is a one-day circuit of the Cap Bon peninsula. It's virtually impossible to cover the same ground by any combination of local buses, but a day's car-hire is a go-it-alone alternative.

Kairouan - about 40 miles away on a good road - is feasible for a half-day trip, starting early before the sun heats up. On a whole-day excursion, there's time to include sightseeing of Sousse and Monastir.

Paying homage to the Romans, a one-day journey features the magnificent remains at Zaghouan, Thuburbo Majus and Dougga.

Southern safaris to the desert South are possible only on two-day or three-day itineraries that normally include the main highlights of El Djem, Gabès, Matmata and the oases around the edges of Chott el Djerid. Some tours are routed via Kairouan, Sbeitla and Gafsa. These trips are operated by air-conditioned coach or mini-bus; or, on the more adventurous versions, by Land Rover.

For pure entertainment, early-evening excursions are made to the oriental folklore show at Sahara City, about 3 miles out of Hammamet. Another evening, you could try a similar frolic at Bellaoum, located this side of Sousse. They are both excellent value, with food and non-stop wine included.

Recommended restaurants

In Hammamet and Nabeul, all the main hotels feature à la carte restaurants. Otherwise, for dining out, take your pick from these:

Le Berbère - in the centre of Hammamet, opposite the entrance to the Medina, with a spectacular terrace view.

La Pergola - a favourite for international cuisine, above the cinema in the Commercial Centre, with indoor or outdoor seating.

La Coupole - on the main road, Hammamet South, good setting with Tunisian entertainment.

Pomodoro - an Italian restaurant on the sea front.

Chinois - for a change of cuisine, Chinese food Tunisian style, opposite Hammamet railway station.

Delphine - specializing in fish.

Sand Pub - among several others in a restaurant complex which includes the Quick-Restaurant Pizzeria at the Commercial Centre, try the Sand Pub's 1st-floor à la carte section. Their specialty of Soufflé aux Crevettes is superb.

L'Olivier - in Nabeul, a favourite pizzeria and restaurant which has won international awards. Try their snails in garlic sauce! Or a turkey steak, flambé'd at the table, with peppers.

If you want a typical Tunisian restaurant which is open all night, but no alcohol, go to Hédi Wali which is normally pronounced by visitors as Heady Wellie's. Located on the Hammamet-Nabeul road.

The Cap Bon circuit

From your holiday base in Hammamet or Nabeul, it's worth taking a whole-day sightseeing tour of the Cap Bon peninsula, giving you a countryside view of Tunisia. Estimate 160 miles for the full circuit around the coastal road, either by self-drive car or - more relaxed - by organised coach tour.

Cap Bon is one of the Republic's richest and greenest areas, with winter and summer climate mellowed by proximity to the sea. There are large orange groves, lemons and mandarines. Local market-garden crops include tomatoes, peanuts, olives, onions, tobacco, strawberries and garlic - all for local sale, or export mainly to France. In food factories, paprika is converted to harissa - the hot, red spice which lurks in so many Tunisian dishes. Wide vineyards produce red, white and rosé wine. Grombalia is the centre of processing and bottling, and holds a wine festival in August.

Some farmers are share-croppers, going 50/50 with a local landowner. School-children get three months' break in summer, when they help parents in the fields.

Animal power is still used - donkeys or small horses for donkey-cart transport or light ploughing. Occasionally you still see camels who haven't yet diversified into tourism - ploughing, drawing water from a well, or hauling carts. Sheep have enormously fat tails, reputedly as a storage of fat for the time when pasturage is short.

Coach-tour sightseeing of Cap Bon often starts with visits to the stone-carving village of Dar Chaabane, just outside Nabeul, closely followed by a stop at the blanket-weaving cooperative at Beni Khiar. The itinerary then stays on highway MC 27 which hugs the coastline through to the lighthouse tip of Cap Bon.

Although Hammamet and Nabeul attract the bulk of suntan business, Cap Bon has many more superb beaches along this east coast - at Korba and Kelibia, for instance. Apart from a major Club Med village at Korba with 1200-bed capacity, and a couple of much smaller holiday villages at Kelibia, tourism development is thirty years behind Hammamet.

Kelibia

A Byzantine fortress, rebuilt by Spaniards and upgraded by the Turks, broods on a hilltop overlooking Kelibia, which began life as a Punic trading post in 9th century BC. The strategic attraction was the superb natural harbour, commanding the narrow Mediterranean waters between Africa and Sicily.

Vessels in the port specialise in night fishing for sardines, anchovies, mackerel and bonito. It's a colourful sight, every boat fitted with green- or blue-painted lamps to lure the fish. The crystal-clear harbour water glints with millions of tiny fry, and even quite substantial shoals of bigger specimens.

Kerkouane

A few miles further along is the Punic city of Kerkouane. The site was discovered only in 1952. Excavations show that the remains are pure Phoenician. After the city was destroyed by Regulus, it was never re-settled by the Romans or the Arabs - unlike other Punic cities such as Carthage, Thuburbo Majus and the rest.

Essentially Kerkouane was a Phoenician industrial town, where they manufactured their famous purple dye from a shell-fish called murex - a kind of mussel or whelk. They had another site on Djerba island, with processing based on the original technology from Tyre and Sidon.

Manufacture depended on a colourless glandular secretion of the murex which turns rich purple when exposed to air. The stench of rotting shell-fish must have been industrial pollution at its worst. But there was big money in deep purple - a fast dye for status-symbol cloth, sold to Rome, Sardinia, Sicily and Greece; or bartered in Cornwall for tin.

Kerkouane is not the easiest site for the layman to grasp. There are no big public buildings, only private houses with rooms outlined by knee-high restored walls. Every home had its own well, and a system of piped hot and cold water to a domestic hip-bath - sometimes a double bath, so that man and wife could soak together. Designs had a sophisticaed touch, similar to those sit-down mini-baths which hotels install when bathroom space is for midgets. Likewise, furnishing was built-in: a space-saving Habitat of benches and shelves set into the thick walls.

Floors were covered in a special mosaic made with small pieces of marble, mixed with ceramic. Colouring showed the purple for which the town was a production centre. The mosaics don't say much. They were merely random patterns, not even stylized - quite different from Roman mosaics, which were the colour documentaries of 2000 years ago. The only exception was a symbol for the dreaded god Tanit.

Theories about the Tanit-worship cult is mostly inspired guesswork, but parents had the pre-NSPCC habit of sacrificing their first-born child. Near the site entrance, children were burned in a circular pit, and their ashes put into urns. These are now preserved in the Bardo Museum, Tunis.

Excavations continue. Foreign archaeological schools get permission to dig so-many square metres, on condition of employing local labour. Visitors must pay 2 dinars for the right to take photographs.

It's a beautiful location, on top of cliffs about a hundred feet high, with cool sea breezes. Some holidaymakers camp on the foreshore for free. There is spring water close by, and campers can cook, fish and maybe eat mussels.

El Haouaria

At the northern tip of Cap Bon is a major lighthouse, signalling to ships where to change course around this corner of Africa. Low-profile on the seashore is the beginning of an underwater pipeline to Italy, pumping natural gas from Algeria. It's only 50 miles to the coast of Sicily.

The nearest village is el Haouaria, where the local people live mainly off agriculture, or work in fish business. A Falcon Festival is held from June 1 to 5 every year, with the falcons hunting quail.

Throughout a season from early November till the end of March, intrepid sportsmen can get licenses to shoot thrushes and starling. These birds commute from Europe, arriving punctually every November for their annual feast of ripe olives, and they stay the winter.

Among the other game in the Cap Bon region is woodcock, partridge, hare and wild boar. The swine irritate farmers by rooting up crops with their snouts. As boar is not an acceptable dish for Moslems, farmers welcome foreign hunters, who also pay out for beaters. It's said that German hunters convert their bag into wild-boar sausages.

Close to El Haouaria, at the tip of the peninsula, are ancient stone quarries that originally were used by the Carthaginians, then later by Romans and Byzantines. From the foreshore of Djebel Sidi Abiod, blocks of stone were shipped across the Bay of Tunis, 12 miles to Carthage. The Romans quarried the stone from above, in what was virtually a stone cliff near the beach. Hundreds of slaves cut down from the top, always in the form of a hollow pyramid, constantly widening the base of the cave as they worked down. After 2000 years, the pick-marks still show clearly.

The style of working created around ninety cave-quarries. Inside one cavern is something like a huge sculpted camel. According to legend, gold is hidden underneath; but the camel's enormous weight has defeated all attempts to reach the treasure. Higher in the hills there are bats in the Djebel, enjoying freehold caves where they can flutter undisturbed.

In this area was played out the final act in the Tunisian campaign of 1943. Tunis itself was captured in May 1943 by the 8th Army. A section of the 8th advanced towards the tip of Cap Bon, where the final German troops were dug in with machine guns on the ridge. Caves were packed with massive supplies of weapons and ammunition, in readiness for a last-ditch stand.

Fortunately for the advance guard of British troops, the German command recognized the strategic hopelessness of their position - cut off by Allied shipping from retreat back to Italy - and surrendered. In a dispatch to Winston Churchill, General Alexander wrote: 'It was an astonishing sight to see long lines of Germans driving themselves in their own transport or in commandeered horse-carts westwards in search of prisoner-of-war cages.'

Sidi Daoud

From El Haouaria a highly scenic road - MC 26 - returns towards Tunis. Off the main road, a turning leads down to the west-coast fishing village of Sidi Daoud. The location is best avoided in May and June, when large-scale slaughter of migrating tuna fish is organised, using a Roman netting technique which is now called the Matanza. The sight, and the smell from the village cannery, could put you off tuna-fish sandwiches for evermore.

Korbous

Korbous is another seaside location, dramatically sited at the foot of a mountain, with the road winding down from the MC 26 highway in a series of bends. Goats perch on 60-degree slopes to watch the passing traffic. Seven hot water mineral springs originally attracted wealthy Romans, and Korbous has remained a favoured spa resort ever since.

Patients stay at Hotel les Sources for the full spa treatment, good for gout, rheumatism, obesity and liver. Otherwise, Korbous is just a pleasant weekend destination for city-dwellers from Tunis, out for the fresh air and the chance to dabble their toes in scalding-hot water - 140°F - which gushes from rocks into the sea.

From Korbous, it's 38 miles back to Hammamet - initially along a narrow but panoramic cliff road. Some parts are just single track with passing places. This can be very exciting when the road is jammed with Sunday-outing traffic from Tunis. After the wine-centre of Grombalia, there's choice of the scenic route MC 27 direct to Nabeul, or the fast GP 1 to Hammamet-South.

4. Tunis and Carthage

Mileage from Tunis: Hammamet & Nabeul 40; Sousse 90; Monastir 100; Kairouan 75; Sfax 170; Gabès 230; Gafsa 220; Tozeur 240; Djerba 320.

Tunis makes a popular one-day excursion from the mainland beach resorts. From Hammamet and Nabeul, the capital is only an hour's drive; from the Sousse and Monastir area, two hours. There's much to see. In the central Medina - the original walled Arab town - is all the fascination of the country's largest bazaar zone: a labyrinth of narrow streets, packed with colourful shopping and sightseeing interest. The Bardo Palace - former luxury home of the Turkish-origin Beys who misruled Tunisia - houses one of the world's finest collections of Roman mosaics.

Many excursions also include a short visit to the few remaining highlights of Carthage, such as the Punic port, Roman Baths and the Theatre where Winston Churchill gave a Victory speech to the troops in 1943. A little spare time is left for wandering through the travel-poster village of Sidi bou Said.

It's a packed programme for a single day. If you want to probe deeper, take the guided excursion to get your bearings; and then return another day or two for more detailed exploration of what interests you most. Public transport access from the coastal resorts is very easy, either by rail or road. But check timetables carefully!

Depending on your depth of interest, why not stay overnight in Tunis? For instance, you may be tempted by the major July-August Carthage International Festival of classic music, ballet and jazz which is held annually at the Roman Theatre. Tunis offers a full range of city hotels, from nil-star up to top business grade. Most of the palatable hotels are tightly grouped along Avenue de France and the Avenue Bourguiba, and the side streets that go south towards the railway station.

For business visitors, the Hilton is the best in Tunis, up on Belvedere hill, peacefully removed from traffic noise, and with a luxury pool for relaxing after the hurly-burly of the centre. Holiday visitors can get much lower weekend room rates. Some motor-coach tours of Tunisia start or finish weekends at the Hilton to take advantage of those favourable tariffs. The Africa Meridian Hotel, downtown, is more convenient for location. But the Hilton runs a free shuttle minibus service to and from the Avenue Bourguiba.

The usual practice on Tunis excursions is to park the coach near the inverted pyramid of Hotel du Lac - you can't miss that unusual landmark! Guides then walk their groups to the Medina, through the souks to the Grand Mosque; and finally return to the coach for transport to the Bardo Museum.

Likewise, that starting-point is excellent for a do-it-yourself tour, only a few minutes' walk from the main railway station, or half a mile from the inter-city bus terminal. The location is called Place d'Afrique, with a large statue of former president Habib Bourguiba on a horse, looking straight up the Avenue Bourguiba towards the Medina.

At this major crossroads, several main directions await your choice. Look towards the Hotel du Lac, apparently designed by the architects as a pyramid, but the builders read the plans upside down. On the corner is a Tourist Information Office, where they give away excellent brochures, advice and a free map of Tunis. This building is also headquarters of the Tunisian National Tourist Office.

If you're bent on shopping, a very large ONAT handicraft store is just along Avenue Mohammed V - a low building on the right-hand side. Even if you're not in buying mood, a visit is well worth while, to see tempting displays of Tunisian crafts from pottery and bird-cages to carpets: everything good quality, fixed prices, no haggling.

Close by, down Avenue Bourguiba - direction of the horse's tail - is the suburban railway line that serves Carthage.

Medina Sightseeing

Start your voyage of discovery into the centuries'-old Arab town by walking up the Avenue Habib Bourguiba. This broad French-built boulevard features a central tree-shaded pedestrian precinct, lively with news kiosks, outdoor cafés and flower stalls. On the left-hand side is a blue and white striped skyscraper: the Africa Meridian Hotel, which over-dominates the surrounding area.

For a light meal, numerous small restaurants are spaced along the main avenue and in the side streets, with very reasonable prices - generally lower, in fact, than in the beach resorts. Opposite the Africa Hotel, for instance, the Bagdad Restaurant is loaded with oriental atmosphere, but with quite tolerable menu prices. On a corner past the Africa Hotel is another large branch of ONAT - Maison de l'Artisanat - which is superb for serious buying of Tunisian handicrafts. Continue straight ahead towards Place de l'Indépendance with French Embassy on the left and the 19th-century Cathedral of St. Vincent de Paul on the right.

All this area is of 19th-century origin, based on the ruling colonial policy of constructing a little provincial France outside the native towns.

Most of the grid-pattern streets, southwards of the main avenue towards the railway station, were named after countries. Geography wasn't the planners' strong point. Rue d'Espagne is north of rue d'Angleterre; Russia Street is wedged between England and Morocco; the most westerly street is dedicated to Sweden. On the north side of the Avenue Bourguiba, many streets are named after cities, from Quebec to Rome; or have since been renamed after statesmen from Garibaldi and Gandhi to Lenin. Elsewhere, patriotic Tunisian dates are favoured as street-names: Avenue of 15 October 1961; Boulevard of 9 April 1938; rue 2 March 1934.

After Independence Square, Avenue Habib Bourguiba funnels into the narrower Avenue de France, with pavement activity growing denser as you reach the old borderline between the French and Arab towns at the Porte de France, otherwise known as Bab el-Bahar. The British Embassy is right there by the Gate of France, on a pedestrian-only square called the Place de la Victoire, 1st June 1955. From here onwards, the calendar turns back 1200 years into the Medina founded on the remains of an old Punic town.

The city layout is traditional Arabic, in total contrast to grid-pattern European. Central focal-point is the Great Mosque, around which the town grew from its foundation in year 732. From the main city gate, High Street Tunis - called Rue Jamaa ez-Zitouna, named after the Mosque of the Olive-Tree - runs direct to the historic place of Friday worship.

That main street is lined entirely with shopkeepers, like Main Street anywhere. In the 20th century of tourism, that means virtually every merchant is pitching for the souvenir trade. Every innocent passerby is accosted in a selection of half a dozen languages, and cajoled into stopping to look inside. Friendly touts implore you to come and visit their uncle's carpet shop, because Uncle so admires the English - or the Germans, or the Swedes, depending on nationality. Many visitors feel harassed by the constant sales pressure. Just ignore it. Don't let it spoil your pleasure in fascinating sightseeing. This is the Orient. A thousand and one details are awaiting your camera lens.

Look, for instance, at No. 55 on the right-hand side - at the heavily-studded wooden door of the periodicals branch of the National Library. Peep inside at the delightful courtyard. Quite close,

up a side turning to the right, and then left, is the main section of the National Library, with another heavy wooden yellow door to admire, and a pattern of massive black metal studs. The inner courtyard, with reading room to one side, is a cool retreat from the hurly-burly of the surrounding souks. The atmosphere is full of quiet Arabic erudition, showing you another aspect of Islam.

Finally, there's the Great Mosque. Hopefully you've arrived in time to enter the courtyard. Visiting hours for non-Moslems are mornings only, from 8 till 12. Since foundation in the 8th century, using recycled columns from more ancient monuments, the building has been greatly enlarged and restored, though much of the original structure remains. In the hierarchy of Islam, the Mosque of the Olive Tree ranks second in Tunisia to Kairouan's Great Mosque.

Why that name? Quite simply, followers were taught by the founder beneath an olive tree that grew on the original site. Then, for almost a thousand years, the Great Mosque doubled as the centre of a theological university, teaching Koranic law and philosophy. That's why the National Library is located only a hundred yards away. The Mosque and the surrounding area was a place of learning long before any university was established in dark-age Europe.

As you face the Great Mosque entrance, the street running left is Booksellers' Row - rue des Libraires - lined on one side with former residential Islamic colleges called Medressas. These followed the classic pattern of student cells around a rectangular courtyard. Even into the 1950's, some 10,000 students were based in Tunis, until theological studies were moved to Kairouan in the 1960's.

Having run the gauntlet of the souvenir shopkeepers of Main Street, you may appreciate the calmer atmosphere of souks closer to the mosque. An occasional vendor smokes his hubble-bubble pipe, and stays in thoughtful mode until aroused by a customer who wants attention. Along the right-hand side of the Great Mosque runs the Souk el-Attarine - Street of the Perfumers - where the bottled scent of flowers, jars of incense and sacks of henna all combine into an aromatic cocktail. Pick your mixture, and the chosen scent can be bottled on the spot.

Continue straight up the Perfumers' Bazaar into the vaulted Souk et-Trouk - the Turkish souk, built in 1630 - and you finally come to Souk el-Berka, which formerly was the Slave Market, in the days when piracy was big business. It's now one of the prettiest streets in the Medina.

On the left-hand side of the Great Mosque is Souk de la Laine which theoretically is a textile bazaar, but is mainly tenanted by jewellers. They offer great choice of silver filigree work. Gold items are sold by weight. Close by, entire vaulted streets display bolts of cloth of every texture and design.

Much enjoyment in the Medina comes from just wandering at random, looking for the unexpected. Venture into the smaller side-streets, more residential in character. Through archways and along cobbled lanes, you'll find many splendid front doors, heavily studded. Specially notice the door knockers, which mostly represent the Hand of Fatima - daughter of the prophet Mohammed - with fingers and thumb extended.

There's magic in the lucky number five. Fatima's Hand, and also the outline drawing of a fish, gives highly effective protection against the evil eye.

You'll certainly stray into workshop areas, where each trade is tightly grouped together. You can watch hat-makers at work, shaping the traditional red chechia which is still worn by middle-aged and elderly men. Elsewhere are the slipper-makers. Working conditions are often like in early days of the Industrial Revolution, somewhere between medieval and Victorian sweat-shop. Many premises have been converted into mini-factories devoted to the booming souvenir trade. Peek discreetly into courtyards, and you'll see machinery which is worthy of an 18th-century industrial museum.

From the Porte de France through to the Great Mosque, the street goes slightly uphill. Behind the Mosque, the incline becomes steeper towards the Kasbah area at the hill-top. Along that route you could easily be lured to sit down and inspect the magnificent displays featured by carpet shops.

To build traffic through their premises, several stores including the Maison de l'Orient invite you to see a panorama of Tunis from their rooftop terraces. There's no harm in accepting the offer, to get best possible view of the gleaming-white rooftops dominated by the 145-ft minaret of the Great Mosque - almost impossible to see from any ground level. Only snag is that you'll be sorely exposed to three floors of carpet temptation as you climb up and down the stairs.

Here's a suggestion for less tiring, downhill sightseeing. If you're making your second visit to the Medina - having already done the guided tour from Porte de France to the Great Mosque - take a cab *direct* to the Kasbah. At the top end of rue de la Kasbah are government offices, including the Prime Ministry, guarded by police, and by soldiers in fancy dress. The next white building along rue de la Kasbah is the Ministry of National Economy. From there, everything goes steadily downhill until you emerge at Porte de France.

Another possibility is to ask the cab-driver to drop you at rue du Chateau, which is close to Place de la Kasbah. This alternative entrance to the Medina opens up a delightful little corner, with a mosque by the gated entrance from the Boulevard Bab Mnara. Facing you is the National Institute for Archaeology and Art - a blue and white building with an elegant front door. To the right is an arched gateway for the continuation of rue du Chateau. The archway looks like a stage set - again with an ochre-coloured door heavily decorated with metal studs. It's visually rewarding to stroll through this quiet residential area at the southern end of the Medina, with its monumental facades, traditional windows, small mosques and shrines - a contrast to the more commercial streets of the Medina.

Tunis transport

Having completed your Medina sightseeing, where else to go in Tunis? From the city centre - that is, from Avenue Bourguiba - the most useful bus services are: No. 3 to The Bardo Museum; Nos. 5 or 7 to Belvedere Park; No. 35 to the Airport. For Carthage, Sidi Bou Said and La Marsa, the TGM Metro railway is easily the best choice of transport.

Otherwise, for shorter distances, taxis are plentiful and low-cost. In fact, a cab-ride is an exciting experience in itself. For the driver, the city traffic represents a constant duel: him against the rest. In the general cut and thrust, all normal traffic rules are ignored. At traffic lights, red means go if he can make it. It's a life full of excitement, in which the passenger can share.

If you aim to visit Carthage, go down Avenue Bourguiba past Place de l'Afrique, signposted as La Goulette. Two blocks past the equestrian statue of Bourguiba is the TGM railway station where a suburban train called the Metro runs every 20 minutes to Carthage: the world's only archaeological site which can be visited by using six stops on a Metro line. The line also continues to Sidi Bou Said and La Marsa. Fares are about 35p first class. It's worth paying the small difference for a 1st-class ticket. Second class is more ethnic and crowded, probably with standing room only unless you're among the first to board.

Bardo Museum

Open 9.30 - 16.30 hrs. Entrance one dinar. Tel. 513650 or 513842. About a half-hour ride by no. 3 bus from Avenue Bourguiba; or much quicker by taxi. Also there are numerous buses from the city Bus Station at Habib Thameur Square - a quarter-mile from Avenue de France, up Rue de Rome. Nos. 4, 16, 23, 30 or 42 all pass by Bardo Museum.

The Bardo is almost overwhelming with its wealth of Roman mosaics. It's like a National Art Gallery of 1600 years ago. Acres of mosaics decorate the walls and floors, like sumptuous tapestries and carpets. When Roman settlers colonized Tunisia, they hit it rich. Vast quantities of grain, olive oil and wine were shipped to Rome, keeping the Imperial capital supplied with bread, fuel for oil-lamps, and drink.

Wherever the Romans settled in Tunisia, they could soon afford to decorate their palatial villas with all the ostentation that money could buy. Mosaics were the equivalent of the paintings, tapestries and carpets of moneyed landowners in later centuries. Happily, mosaics do not fade, and suffer little damage even if buried for a thousand years. Today they provide a unique colour documentary of the hedonistic Roman life-style in Tunisia during the golden age of the 1st to 3rd centuries AD.

Virtually every Roman site in Tunisia has yielded up mosaics; and, to a lesser extent, statues. The cream of these treasures are housed in the Bardo, leaving the sites relatively bare. Thus, for the layman, it's best to visit the Bardo first, before trailing around Roman remains in the countryside. You can then colour the dusty sites with your imagination, re-creating mosaic floors, wall decorations, statues, and all the smaller items like oil-lamps, wine-jars, weapons and household crockery.

At Carthage, for instance, there are no statues left on the scattered sites - just the remaining bits and pieces of walls, columns and plinths. It's difficult for the non-expert to conjure up a mental picture of the original city and its public monuments. But the Bardo Museum has a good collection of statuary which can flesh out your impressions.

However, for most visitors, it's the mosaics which are the most memorable. They still sparkle with life, illustrating every aspect of a Roman settler's enjoyment of sport, hunting, fishing, fighting, love-making, feasting and especially drinking. Their favourite god was Bacchus, usually depicted at least half drunk.

The mosaics were not necessarily produced by great artists. Many of the figures would be dismissed as crude caricatures by an art critic. Often, animals look as though copied straight from a child's painting book.

A typical 2nd-century mosaic depicts Orpheus, charming the beasts with his divine music. While Orpheus plays, various animals stand around looking cheerful and enchanted, from the tiger and lion, to the goat, horse, cow and monkey. Even the birds participate in what seems like a general sing-song.

But mostly the animals were there to be hunted or eaten, unless they were lucky enough to have a Christian for lunch at the circus. Blood in the gladiator and hunting scenes was usually pictured by splodges falling down like red spaghetti.

Long before the days of over-fishing, the Tunisian waters were crammed with seafood, judging by mosaics that depict almost more fish than water. The Romans obviously enjoyed a fish dinner, with the menu choice little different from today, even down to the humble octopus. Fishing methods are well documented. A typical 3rd-century mosaic depicts 23 fishing vessels, giving a detailed idea of boat design from 1700 years ago. One of the largest mosaics is 'The Triumph of Neptune', packed with scenes from the god's sparkling underwater life. He drives a chariot drawn by sea-horses, while his wife Amphritite prefers to ride the waters nude with her arm around a galloping sea tiger.

Favourite deities and legendary characters made good subjects. The

41

Four Seasons were always popular, with Apollo to supervise. The Muses were likewise greatly favoured, sometimes three, sometimes nine, depending on the floor space available. A splendid mosaic from near Zaghouan shows deities presiding over the seven days of the week; and, all around, the 12 signs of the zodiac. There are mosaics of Centaurs, who show what happens if mother loves horses too much, or if father has somewhat off-beat sexual tendencies. From Dougga comes a mosaic depicting Odysseus tied to the mast of his vessel, while listening to the song of the Sirens.

Probably one hour is the limit to what most people can take of room after room of mosaics. Best policy is then just to abandon the rest and come back another day; or to buy a coffee-table book of reproductions at the exit, and admire the mosaics at leisure back home.

In fact the Bardo Museum also includes a Punic section, though much more limited in scope. After the pop-art displays of Roman mosaics, it's hard for the non-archaeologist to get excited about the modest figurines from Punic times, though you can still thrill to the grotesque Punic masks of terra-cotta.

At the same time, look at the Bardo Museum from the viewpoint of its original function as the Palace and Harem of the Beys. Most of the rooms still retain their original Turkish-type decoration with tiles and stucco work, lofty ceilings and chandeliers.

This prepares you for the total contrast of entering the museum's Oriental section. Whereas the Romans pictured every form of animal and human life, the Moslem tradition is that all representation of living things is akin to idolatry. Hence the Islamic genius for non-representational art, shown in their decoration of tiles or carpets. It comes almost as a relief after the overwhelming exuberance of the Roman style.

Sharing the same grounds as the Bardo Museum is the National Assembly - the Tunisian Parliament. It's a modest-looking building. Sentries in traditional red toy-soldier uniform guard the entrance staircase. They look like something out of Madame Tussauds, until you find they move. The staircase is also defended by eight stone lions, all looking eager for strangers to eat.

Carthage

In Britain, we know relatively little about the Punic peoples. They came as Carthaginian or Phoenician traders, bartering purple cloth for Cornish tin, and had Punic Wars numbered 1st, 2nd and 3rd. Our school histories have very brief chapters on Punic civilization, in contrast to their coverage of Greek and Roman. See Chapter 13 of this book for a capsule reminder.

The reputed founder of Carthage was Elissa, a fugitive princess from the Phoenician city of Tyre. She led an adventure-packed life. After her husband was murdered by her brother, Pygmalion, she escaped to Cyprus and thence journeyed to present-day Tunisia. She made a shrewd land-purchase deal with the local chief, called Iarbas, and established the trading city of Carthage.

When the settlement flourished, Iarbas wanted to marry Elissa, threatening war if she refused. To escape this offer of marriage, and to save her country

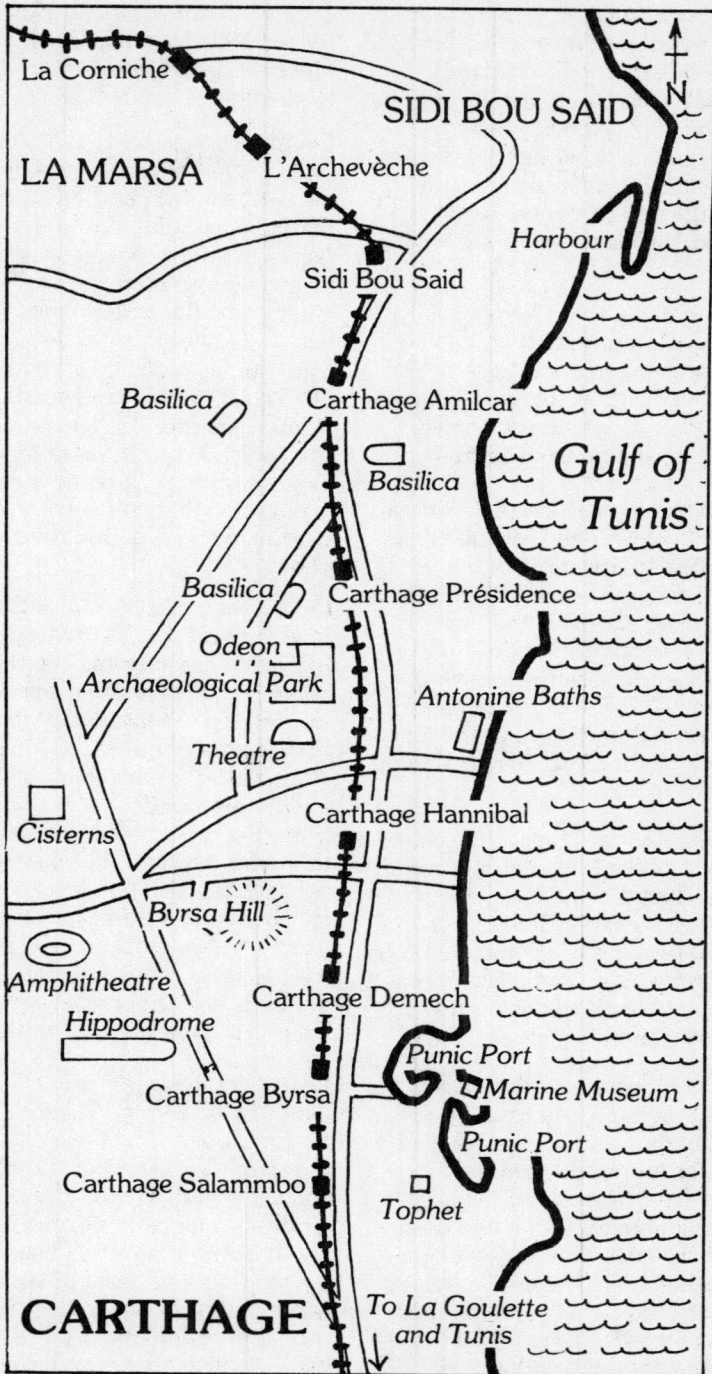

La Corniche

SIDI BOU SAID

LA MARSA

L'Archevèche

Harbour

Sidi Bou Said

Basilica

Carthage Amilcar

Gulf of
Tunis

Basilica

Basilica

Carthage Présidence

Odeon

Archaeological Park

Antonine Baths

Theatre

Cisterns

Carthage Hannibal

Byrsa Hill

Amphitheatre

Hippodrome

Carthage Demech

Punic Port

Carthage Byrsa

Marine Museum

Punic Port

Carthage Salammbo

Tophet

CARTHAGE

To La Goulette
and Tunis

from the ordeal of war, Elissa ordered a funeral pyre to be built, and stabbed herself to death. The Roman epic poet, Virgil, switched the story and the chronology in his Aeneid, and renamed Elissa as Dido. In his version of the legend, Dido fell in love with Aeneas - the son of Venus - and committed suicide when he deserted her.

However, despite that fate of its founder, Carthage flourished, built a great trading empire, and became the main rival of Rome. Likewise, the centre of Phoenician power shifted from Tyre, to the new power base of Carthage. At its peak, the Carthaginian empire included Tunisia, the coast of Algeria and Morocco, southern Spain, and most of the central Mediterranean islands: Malta, Sicily, Sardinia, Corsica and the Balearics. The confrontation with Roman power, across the straits of Messina in 270 BC, led ultimately through three Punic Wars to the final destruction of the Carthaginian city by the Romans in 146 BC.

Even on the spot in Tunisia, the Punic department of the National Museum is really very limited. The Carthaginians were the top people in Tunisia for almost 700 years; but a combination of Roman destruction, Vandals and time have removed most traces of this ancient civilization.

Likewise in Carthage itself. There's really not much to see except their burial grounds, and the sanctuary of Tanit where first-born children were sacrificed. Two lagoons by the shore have been identified as the two ports of Hannibal's city - one for warships, and the other for merchant vessels. Nearly everything that survived the centuries is totally Roman. The principal exception is the recently excavated area of Punic Housing on Byrsa Hill, where the Carthage Museum and a 19th-century Cathedral are located.

On most coach tours that do Tunis and Carthage in a day, it's usual to visit just the Roman Baths of Antoninus. Going round the Carthage National Museum may seem lack-lustre after an hour has earlier been spent amid the brilliant mosaics of the Bardo. However, on a one-language tour, some guides do stop at the Punic Houses in the Museum enclosure. The Roman Theatre is often viewed from the coach, but without getting off to explore on foot. In truth, a single day is not enough to see all that Tunis, Carthage and Sidi Bou Said have to offer.

On a do-it-yourself tour of Carthage, bear in mind that the principal highlights are extremely spread-out. It could be worth hiring a self-drive car for the day. Alternatively, check the map for the handiest TGM rail stations to the sites you wish to visit, and be prepared for plenty of walking. Some sectors can be reached by thumbing any taxi that happens to pass by. It's also possible to save your legs by hiring a horse-carriage at Carthage Hannibal station, but it's wise to reach complete agreement first on the price. Otherwise, your pocket instead of your feet will ache.

If your choice is rail and shoe-leather, get out at Carthage Salammbo station for the Tophet and the Punic Ports; Carthage Dermech for the Museum and Punic Housing on Byrsa Hill; Carthage Hannibal for the Theatre and the Antonin Baths. Carthage Byrsa is not the best station for reaching the Byrsa; in fact, that station is closest to the Military Port. Put on good walking shoes, and allow a full day to cover the main points. The intervening sectors make interesting walking, through very wealthy garden suburbs that include the presidential palace.

To visit modern-day Carthage, let's start with the TGM train ride from Tunis out to the suburbs.

First the train rattles across a causeway over a lagoon called the Lake of Tunis. A canal alongside the causeway enables ocean-going ships to dock in Tunis port. Fishermen in small boats can sometimes be seen using an age-old method of casting a net and hoping to make a catch. Watch out for flamingoes, who likewise are hoping to catch a fish.

La Goulette is the first train-stop on the coast. The French place-name means 'gullet' or 'throat', to describe the constricted entrance from the sea into the lagoon. Tunis residents often stop here for a fish meal. There are many fish restaurants at La Goulette, but otherwise this suburban town is not worth making a special journey. However, for anyone with time for more sightseeing, the grim kasbah was formerly used as a warehouse for Christian captives who were awaiting sale as slaves if they had no potential for ransom. During peak periods, the kasbah had 10,000 slaves in stock.

Next station is Goulette Neuve, a commuter suburb. Then comes Goulette Casino, but you're wasting your time if you want to gamble, for there is no casino. Aéroport is somewhat similar: it has no airport. (Seaplanes used to land close by). But the next stop, Carthage-Salammbo, is for sightseers who want to visit the Tophet of Salammbo, the most ancient Punic place of worship. The entrance is on rue Hannibal.

Its history is gruesome. The French novelist, Gustave Flaubert, created highly-coloured descriptions of the macabre rites as new-born children were hurled by dedicated priests into a furnace. But archaeologists agree that the basic facts were true enough - that children were regularly sacrificed as an offering to the god, Moloch. The ashes were then placed in urns, and buried in layers marked by inscribed gravestones, technically known as *cippi* or votive steles. Later, under the Romans, the site was used for a number of purposes, including ovens for pottery manufacture.

Close by is the merchant harbour of the two lagoon ports of Carthage. Maybe, some time in the future, resources will be devoted to full excavation and restoration of these Carthaginian docks which were the base for the greatest trading empire of antiquity. Meanwhile, all you see is just two stretches of muddy swamp. Near the military harbour, just north of the merchant harbour, are models made by a British team who worked on a UNESCO project to safeguard the site.

An Oceanographic Museum is located between the two ports; but shed no tears if the building is closed. Frankly, it's not very thrilling. Carthage Byrsa is an alternative train-stop, closest to the Punic ports.

Then comes Carthage Dermech, which is a convenient station for access to Carthage Museum and Punic Housing. From the station, cross the railway line and go straight up the hill, called Avenue Titelive. The avenue is lined with spacious villas, set in luxuriant gardens, dripping with bougainvillaea. Swing away uphill, to the right - always keep climbing - until you see the dome of the Cathedral.

45

That's the main landmark, pointing your way to the Museum. At the end of the road, take the concrete steps that lead up to the left.

To catch your breath, stop at the charming Hotel la Reine Elyssa Didon, for refreshment on the terrace. Hotel Didon has 22 rooms, a pleasant Tunisian atmosphere and a reputation for good food, besides being very handy for exploring Carthage. All this uphill climb is well worth the effort, to give a view of the present 20th-century development of luxury villas down the hill slopes of ancient Carthage. Near the shoreline is the President's Palace. You can see why wealthier Tunisians enjoy living in this prestige residential area, with a commuter train every 20 minutes into town. A superb panoramic view overlooks the Gulf of Tunis to the mountain peaks of Cap Bon across the water.

The Museum is another 600 yards away, with entrance to the grounds just past the Cathedral - an unloved building, shut for repair. The metal doors are rusted, and many of the stained glass windows are broken.

The Archaeological Museum was formerly headquarters of the White Fathers, who undertook some of the original site excavations in late 19th century. All these grounds formed the hilltop acropolis both of Punic and Roman Carthage. Here was the reputed setting for the deal by which Queen Dido gained possession of land for building the original city.

According to legend, when Dido arrived as a refugee from Tyre, she offered to buy from the locals as much land as she could enclose in a bull's hide. The locals jumped at the offer, thinking that a bull's hide couldn't enclose very much.

But they were out-smarted by the Phoenicians. Dido cut the skin into very narrow strips, tied them end to end, and encircled an area which stretched from the sea to the hilltop. Hence the name according to Greek and Roman legend: Byrsa, meaning bull's hide. In fact, Byrsa was probably a Punic word, which may have meant something like citadel.

Since then, modern archaeologists have knocked holes in the legend. In fact, the Byrsa hill was not inhabited at all during the city's early period. More likely, Byrsa was used just like any other hill around the city - namely as a place of burial during the 7th and 6th centuries BC. The area then was left unused until the 4th century BC, when the Byrsa was occupied by iron and copper metal-working shops. Finally, some time around 180 BC, a residential area was developed on the hillside slopes. These houses were destroyed with the rest of the Punic town in 146 BC. The site was then left abandoned for more than a century, while natural forces slowly modified the appearance of the destroyed quarter.

When Rome decided to rebuild Carthage in Roman style, they chose the Byrsa as their city-plan centre. The top of the hill was shaved off and the slopes were covered with fill as much as 7 metres thick. Essentially the Byrsa hill was levelled into a plateau. The remains of Punic housing, buried beneath the landfill, became part of the foundation and platform for Roman buildings: the Forum and the monumental centre with temples and later a basilica.

After the Arab conquest at the end of the 7th century, the site at first was abandoned. Roman building materials were carted off for any construction project that needed readymade columns and dressed stone. However, the remains of various walls, reservoirs and ceramics are proof of sporadic habitation which continued until the 16th century.

Much has been revealed during more recent times, especially thanks to a UNESCO 'Save Carthage Campaign' from 1974 onwards. All this area is protected as part of the National Park of Carthage and Sidi Bou Said. The aim is to preserve the sites which reflect 3000 years of North African history. Numerous excavations are being undertaken around the Carthage area by a dozen archaeological schools from different countries.

A French team from Grenoble was assigned the Byrsa. By removing the 23 feet depth of landfill, the French have been able to reconstruct an area of Punic city as at the time of destruction in 146 BC. The excavations have revealed blocks of residential houses, dated between 180 to 146 BC - the very last period of Punic habitation. Archaeologists suggest that this was a government development for civil servants or priests.

These housing blocks are built on streets which meet at right-angles; and the blocks are all built to two standard sizes - evidence of a planned development. The streets are stepped up the Byrsa's one-in-six slope. Hence there was never any wheeled traffic up these streets, only pedestrians and perhaps donkeys.

The French archaeologists left what look like tall pillars of earth in between the housing blocks. They indicate the 23-ft depth of the Roman land-fill, and demonstrate how the remains of the Punic houses were preserved by their burial.

The houses were on a very simple plan, mostly with a corridor running from the street to a courtyard with small rooms opening off that central courtyard. Access to upper storeys was probably by rope ladders, wooden staircases or perhaps by steps that came up from the street.

Carthage is the site in North Africa with the poorest natural spring water supply. Every house had its individual cistern for rainwater collection, in the typical bathtub shape of Punic design. Each cistern was fitted with a characteristic gabled lid, and a manhole so that the householder could go down and periodically clean it out.

According to a historian's description of the siege of Carthage in 146 BC, the Romans, as they fought their way up the hill, encountered houses which were six storeys high. That was probably an exaggeration, but experts reckon the buildings were at least two or three storeys tall. One clue is that the exterior walls are very thick and would have supported a number of storeys. On the site itself, you can see some of the Punic building techniques first-hand. For instance walls were made with pillars, and rubble packed in between, to cut down on the use of cut stone.

It's best to visit the Museum first, to get an overall interpretation of the site and its layout and history. The Museum is arranged in four main sections: Prehistoric, Punic, Roman and Early Christian. The adjoining garden is the peaceful setting for a collection of Roman columns, statues, bits of masonry and stone sarcophagi.

Then go to the terrace and steps overlooking the Punic Housing - and enjoy the splendid contrast of 2100 years in a single viewpoint. In the foreground are the foundations and walls of the Punic houses. Less than a hundred yards further down the terraced hillside are luxury white villas with TV dish aerials on their flat rooves.

Due west of Carthage Museum - away from the sea and on the outskirts of the original city - are the remains of two major Roman sites: the Cisterns of **La Malga** and the **Amphitheatre**.

The huge Cisterns were built to store water brought by the Roman-engineered aqueduct that ran from Zaghouan, 44 miles away, to supply the water needs of a city of some 700,000 people.

The amphitheatre, close by, was the scene of several martyrdoms of early Christians, torn apart by wild animals. The structure was used as a stone quarry over the centuries, and only the foundations remain. Before the building was torn apart by enterprising quarrymen, it rivalled the Colosseum of Rome with 36,000 seating capacity. It's hard to believe that a building of such size could just disappear.

The adjoining **Circus** suffered a similar fate, and there's very little to see except a couple of humps where spectators sat to watch the chariot races. If time is short, the visitor doesn't miss much by skipping this area of old-time Carthage.

Closer to the Byrsa Hill - due north, except that the access roads wind around - is the 2nd-century **Hadrian's Theatre**, which should not be missed. Of course, most of the original stage buildings and roof have long since vanished - that process having been started by the Vandals, enjoying their hobby of destruction. For centuries the ruins were home to squatter-type villagers. Twentieth-century excavations have revealed rich ornamentation and statuary, now housed in the Bardo Museum. Since then, the seating has been reconstructed with new stone slabs, so that the 5,000-capacity theatre lives again every summer for the Carthage Festivals and a varied programme of music and theatre performances.

On the hill behind the Roman Theatre was the smaller but covered **Odeon**, which similarly was levelled by the Vandals, so that only the foundations remain. An adjoining heap of rubble from the ruins offers an overall view of modern Carthage and its scattered archaeology.

In the same area, just below the viewpoint, is the Archaeological Park of the **Odeon Villas** - a Roman residential area, with Punic, Roman and Byzantine antiquities. There's a paved street with the foundations of Roman villas, and an **Antiquarium** based on the remains of a large villa with an enviable panoramic view of the Gulf of Tunis.

The most impressive Archaeological Park is linked with the **Baths of Antoninus**, located next door to the Presidential Palace. These fantastic Baths covered a floor space of 9 acres, and certainly rank among the most important in the Roman world. Building began during Emperor Hadrian's reign (118 to 138) and construction was completed during the reign of Antoninus Pius (138 to 161 AD). The Baths continued in use until the end of the Roman era. Afterwards, in the usual way, they served as a stone quarry, handily placed by the shore for sea transport. During the 19th century, the British Navy joined in the general looting, and the swag can be seen today in the British Museum.

So, for all these reasons of destruction, neglect and shipment of anything moveable, only the basement foundations remain - but those foundations are mind-boggling enough. Numerous sculptures have been recovered, and are now safe in the Bardo Museum. A marble plaque on a terrace overlooking the site gives an artist's impression of the original grandeur of the building. From that location, you can trace the size and location of the various rooms of the baths, from the entrance to the changing-room, to the warm bath, the massage room, the steam or sweating room, the tepidarium, and the cold-water frigidarium; then an Olympic-size swimming pool and a gymnasium. A healthy lot, the Romans!

Sidi Bou Said

Located 12 miles from Tunis, and perched on a rocky spur 400 feet above the shoreline, Sidi Bou Said is almost impossibly picturesque. Everywhere you point a camera comes out as another chocolate-box view: cobbles, blue doors, Moorish arches, delicate window grilles, heavily-studded patterned doors, and brilliant whitewashed houses, cube-shaped with flat rooves.

Dominating the main street is the great travel-poster scene, taking in the flight of steps leading up to the Moorish tea-house called Café des Nattes. This view is regarded as 'typical' of Tunisia. In fact, it's hard to find anywhere else that is nearly so picturesque. The closest attempt to reproduce the setting is at Port El Kantaoui.

The Café des Nattes is laid out in Moorish style. Customers sit cross-legged on rush mats and smoke a friendly hookah or narghile, or drink their coffee or tea. Remarkably, despite the huge attraction to shoals of tourists, prices in the village are not out of line. At a typical central restaurant, one cannot grumble at the menu prices. Stalls sell every possible combination of nuts, dates, loukum, helva, nougat and other sticky sweets. There's the usual line of souvenir stores.

Traditionally, Sidi Bou Said was production centre for very attractive bird cages. Designs and colours are lively, reproducing the patterns of Arabic architecture: doorways, arches, domes, minarets. Nowadays, these are bought more often for their potential as flower holders; or as decorative lighting fixtures in hallways or summer gardens. Larger models are used for fanciful displays in department stores or restaurants. All these birdcages capture the light and airy spirit of Sidi Bou Said, with its white buildings, blue doorways and grillwork windows. Production is now bigger than ever before, with massed birdcages in souvenir shops everywhere in Tunisia, and a thriving export trade. But manufacture has moved away from the village itself.

Essentially, craft workshops can no longer afford premises in Sidi Bou Said, which has become very up-market residential. Climb the hilly side-streets, just one or two terraces higher, and you arrive into a world of elegance and sophistication. Old-time village houses have been tastefully converted into fashionable dwellings. Apart from residents' vehicles, no traffic is permitted within the village, and you can enjoy the sound of bird-song, whether caged or not.

At the hill-top, near a lighthouse on the cliff edge, a cool breeze wafts up the cliff-face. If you decide to stay overnight, a simple and central hotel called the Dar Said offers moderate room rates. It has a somewhat faded appearance, but is full of atmosphere and bougainvillaea.

From the central main street of Sidi Bou Said, steps lead down the cliffside to the harbour with a mixture of pleasure craft - some very luxurious - and an honest working fleet of fishing boats. In late afternoon the fishermen prepare nets for their night-time departure, fishing by lamplight.

Next to the harbour is a small, but very broad beach of golden sand, lightly decorated with litter. Facing the port is a businessman's restaurant called Les Pirates, highly rated for fish. Another good restaurant is the Phenicien, which is part of the Residence Africa holiday apartments, run by the same group as the Africa Hotel in Tunis.

Further round the bay, Hotel Hamilcar adjoins a fine stretch of golden sand, forested with umbrellas. At this hotel, electric current is 110 volts. It's a good base for any enthusiast wanting to explore the archaeology of Carthage in fine detail. The Metro station is 250 yards from the hotel, with trains that run from 6 a.m. till midnight - into Tunis, or further out to Sidi Bou Said and La Marsa.

In La Marsa, the place to go during summer months is the Saf-Saf café-restaurant, famed for its completely Tunisian style cuisine. As an additional attraction, the café also features a traditional camel-powered well, which is pictured on postcards and tourist promotions. During high-season summer months, it's hard to find a spare table. The seating is filled not just with tourists, but mainly with Tunis city-dwellers who take the train out for a breath of seaside air. It's a

well-established tradition. Formerly, the Beys of Tunis would move their court to La Marsa during summer, and top diplomats followed. The British ambassador's residence was used as Field Marshall Alexander's headquarters after the liberation of Tunis in May 1943.

Finally, the last outpost of Tunis suburbs within easy commuter range is Gammarth, another luxury residential area with several high-grade hotels and restaurants. Considerable development is planned for the future, to include a first-class casino and a Centre d'Animation. La Baie des Singes - Monkeys' Bay - takes its name from earlier use of the beach by nudists. Local spectators commented: 'They look like monkeys!'

Restaurants of Tunis

Auberge Alsacienne, 6 Rue
Angleterre   Tel. 246615

Belvedere, Tunis Hilton   Tel. 782800

Capitole, 60 Ave Habib
Bourguiba   Tel. 246601

Carcasonnais, 8 Ave de
Carthage   Tel. 256768

Carthage, 10 Rue Ali Bach
Hamba   Tel. 255614

Chez Nous, 5 Rue Marseille
                          Tel. 243043

Erriadh, 9 Rue Ibn Khaldoun
                          Tel. 246516

Gondole, 4 Rue Caire   Tel. 256729

Grill, 17 Ave Habib Bourguiba
                          Tel. 246587

Huchette, 20 Rue Marseille
                          Tel. 349408

Hungaria, 11 Rue Ali Bach
Hamba   Tel. 245469

Malouf, 108 Rue Yougoslavie
                                   Tel. 243180

Mamma (Pizzeria), 11 Bis Rue
  Marseille   Tel. 241256

Milanais, 20 Rue Inde   Tel. 288064

Mon Village, 1 Rue Royaume Arabie
  Seoudite   Tel. 891633

M'Rabet, Souk Ettrouk   Tel. 261729

Orient, 7 Rue Ali Bach Hamba
                                   Tel. 242058

Palais, 8 Ave Carthage   Tel. 256326

Paradiso, 16 Ave Etats Unis
  Amerique   Tel. 786863

Strasbourg, 100 Rue Yougoslavie
                                   Tel. 241139

5. Sahel – the Central Coast

Sousse

Mileage from Sousse: Tunis 90; Hammamet & Nabeul 60; Monastir 12; Kairouan 35; Mahdia 45; Sfax 80; Gabès 165; Tozeur 220.

A word you'll often meet is Sahel. It means the seashore, and is applied to the olive-rich coastal strip between Sousse and Sfax. The Sahel's principal holiday zone runs from Monastir through Skanès-Plage to Sousse and Port El Kantaoui. Monastir airport, built 1969, handles all the charter-flight traffic into the area. Sousse - focal point of the beach developments - is Tunisia's third largest city.

Sousse was originally settled in 9th century BC by the Phoenicians, and the port became the largest in Africa during Roman times. In late 3rd century AD, the town became a Byzantine capital, renamed Justinianopolis in honour of Emperor Justinian. When the Arabs took over in early 9th century, the present-day layout was established - city walls, Kasbah, Great Mosque and the fortified monastery called the Ribat.

In Sousse, some 40 or 50 holiday hotels are spread for several miles north of the city, including a few within a short walk of the centre. Offering good choice through all grades, from 2-star up to 4-star de luxe, the hotels are well spaced with large garden and pool areas. There are no holiday developments in south Sousse, which is the industrial zone.

Parallel to the beach hotels is a secondary line of shops, bars and restaurants. Many giftware stores employ a resident craftsman by the doorway, chiselling at a pile of copper trays. It encourages passing holidaymakers to stop for a photo, and then be tempted into the store itself, feeling assured that the wares are true local handicrafts, not imported from Taiwan.

Further back from the shoreline, you get closer to the eternal Tunisia. Buses and taxis go speedily into the commercial heart of Sousse, with plentiful sightseeing interest. Like in most Tunisian cities, Sousse is split into two parts - the walled Medina and the mainly French-type centre. In the Medina are the souks with their traditional-style shopping. At the open-air Sunday market, 6.30 a.m. till midday, you can buy woolly camels and other necessities, second-hand clothes or a used set of false teeth.

For self-caterers there are three main supermarkets in Sousse: Monoprix, on Avenue Bourguiba near Sousse Palace Hotel; Magasin Général, behind the Sousse Palace; and Magasin Moderne, near the El Hanna Beach Hotel. Although choice is limited compared with back home, you can find most items at fixed prices, with no need to haggle. Otherwise Medina souks are usually open from 8.30 a.m. till at least 7 p.m., seven days weekly.

The traffic hub of Sousse is a litter-strewn central square - Place Farhat Hached - revolving around a town clock. The litter is swept up early morning, ready for fresh deposits during the day. This square is the main set-down and pick-up point for coaches on city sightseeing tours. A public bus terminal is located beside the port. By the main gate of the medina is starting point for shared-taxi louages to Monastir. Railway trains trundle cautiously across the square with clanging of bells. Even so, visitors aren't usually prepared for a mainline train to clank across the equivalent of Piccadilly Circus, so look both ways when crossing the open track.

The large modern building, facing onto the square, is the Central Bank of Tunisia. If you're stuck for money at the weekend, a list is displayed showing where tourist exchange deals can be handled on Saturdays and Sundays - mostly within a hundred yards of the square. Café and restaurant prices on the main square are about double those which you can find along the popular Avenue Bourguiba, which cuts through from the centre to the beach promenade of Boujaffar. The final quality of the food is much the same.

The principal city gate is right there, with a Martyrs Memorial by the entrance. The Memorial commemorates a revolt against the French, during which demonstrators were shot. The 9th-century town walls are in excellent shape, all around the historic Medina, looking like a film set. The two most important monuments - Great Mosque and the Ribat - are sited just inside the city gate, so you can't miss them. The city Museum is located at the Kasbah, the highest point of the ramparts, at the topmost end of town. Christian catacombs and the Sunday market are close to the Kasbah, but outside the walls.

Entry prices are about 50p each for the Ribat and the Catacombs; 65p for the Museum of Sousse. Permission to photograph costs £1.30 in each of these places. Opening times of the Museum, the Ribat and the Catacombs are from 9-12 and 14-17.30 hrs during the period October to March inclusive; and 9-12 and 15 to 18.30 hrs from April till the end of September.

The most painless way of viewing the sights is to take the special Sunday-morning circuit sponsored by the local Syndicat d'Initiative, with entrance fees included. At the Kasbah entrance, a six-piece Tunisian band and a flag-waver welcome visitors to the Museum collection of Roman mosaics. Close by is the Sunday market. Coach transport takes groups to the central square for a walking tour of Great Mosque, Ribat and the Medina. At the Koubba - a 10th-century building which originally was an Islamic school or medrese - the restored building with a curious fluted roof is used for tourist shows to give a tame idea of a Tunisian wedding.

Great Mosque

Entrance to the Great Mosque is from 9 till 14 hours by ticket costing about 20p, bought from the white-domed Syndicat d'Initiative office on the central Place. If you're organising your own sightseeing, make sure you buy your ticket first - otherwise you'll have to walk back to get it! The Great Mosque is the building with fortress-like walls, with rounded corner turrets, all dating from 850 and little changed since then. Non-Moslems are permitted entrance to the courtyard, but admission to the prayer hall is roped off. However, the doors are left wide open, offering a view of all the 78 columns, with the floor covered in rush mats.

From alongside the Great Mosque there's a splendid view of the Ribat across a charming pedestrian precinct stiff with souvenir stores and boutiques.

The Ribat

The Ribat - a fortified Islamic monastery - was the first of the major Arab buildings, erected by the Aghlabite rulers in 821 AD on a Byzantine site. At the entrance, where a cashier sells admission tickets, a hole in the ceiling was architect-designed for pouring boiling oil onto unwelcome visitors. Warrior monks lived and meditated in spartan cells around the courtyard. Steps lead to the first floor, where accommodation was more spacious. Over the entrance is the original 9th-century prayer hall with ten central pillars, arches each side, and arrow-slits on the outward-facing wall.

A walk around the broad parapets offers good views of the street life below, and across flat rooves which bristle with TV aerials. Climbing the Ribat tower demands the energy for 74 steps up a claustrophobic spiral. Over 11 centuries after being built, it came most useful for aircraft spotting during the North African campaign, when Sousse and the vital port installations were heavily bombed by the Allies.

The Medina

Pass between the Great Mosque and the Ribat, bearing away to the left and you enter rue d'Angleterre - a very narrow street lined with handicraft stores. Just follow the main stream along, where the crowds are thickest and the shopkeepers multilingual. Just anything you want is there, from carpets to bird-cages and hubble-bubble pipes. On sale are traditional handicrafts from villages in the region of Sousse and Monastir: Ksar Hellal for weaving of silk, wool and cotton cloth - particularly the silk scarves worn as a women's headdress; embroidery; pottery, berber costume and solid silver jewelry from Moknine. Haggling is essential. The parallel rue de Paris offers similar shopping potential.

Don't worry about getting lost if you wander off into quieter bazaars, or even along purely residential alleys. Sooner or later you'll pick up the main stream again. Follow the shops, and you'll finally emerge at one of the city gates. Downhill returns you to the port area; uphill finally brings you to the Kasbah and its splendid Museum of Roman mosaics.

As you drift around, there are hundreds of tiny details to notice. Look at the house door-knockers, for instance. Or notice that many of the sticky cakes that are sold from street stalls are now cellophane-wrapped, doing the local flies out of a meal. Try spotting the occasional bit of Roman column, built into a house wall. Everyone's eye is caught by something totally different.

The Kasbah and Museum

In 844 AD the Arab conquerors built the hilltop Kasbah, adding the 100-ft-high signal tower in 859. Today the building is still in active use as the town Museum.

Entrance to the Museum is outside the city wall. From within the medina, go out from a city gate and walk uphill round the ramparts to the dominant Kasbah which looms against the skyline. Most of the Museum is devoted to a superb collection of Roman mosaics.

Just inside the entrance is a tranquil open courtyard, planted with trees and shrubs. Around the courtyard are several mosaics depicting horses in very spirited poses; and then a selection of Roman and Christian epitaphs, dating mainly from 4th century AD. In a little side courtyard is a splendid Medusa, the lady who wore snakes as a hair-do.

A magnificent hall opens from the first courtyard. A superbly crafted mosaic depicts men and women in flirtatious mood, with their clothes in process of removal. Another shows Bacchus being hauled in a chariot by a team of four tigers, like an Esso advertisement.

Fishing scenes reflect the riches of maritime life off the Tunisian shores - something which hasn't changed over the centuries. The mosaics could be used today to decorate an up-market fish restaurant. A typical mosaic panel looks like a four-colour illustration from a coffee-table book: 'Fishes of the Mediterranean.' Anyone who knows his fish could easily identify every one.

So it continues, room after room of lively mosaic documentaries that record every detail of Roman life-style. Unlike Kodachrome, their colours never fade: costume, weaponry, housing, food and drink, entertainment, sport, hunting and debauchery.

In the large central courtyard are almond trees, apricots, peaches, date-palms and fig trees. Roman carvings and inscriptions lean against the wall, along with broken columns which have escaped local housebuilders during the intervening centuries. Occasional small exhibitions of contemporary art are arranged in side rooms. The kasbah ramparts offer good views over the Medina, with its narrow streets leading down to the sea. Cats in 57 varieties sunbathe on rush mats or comfortable doorsteps.

Catacombs

Close to the kasbah, three groups of Christian catacombs have been discovered. These are catacombs of Bon Pasteur - the Good Shepherd - which are open to the public; and catacombs of Hermes (used during the 3rd century), and the catacombs of Sévère (4th century). Bon Pasteur comprises 105 galleries, a mile in total length, containing about 6000 tombs. The catacomb of Hermes accommodated about 2500 tombs, and that of Sévère nearly 5000.

Many finds from these catacombs are housed in the Museum of Sousse, where they can be examined at leisure. Most of the tombs carried epitaphs - some traced in black carbon on tiles, others engraved with the point of a tool, or sometimes even with a finger in a thin covering of limewash applied on the tile. Others were engraved on a marble plaque, or were inscribed in mosaic.

Sousse Museum also features an excavated Punic tomb, dating from 3rd century BC, together with a number of pottery artefacts, such as oil lamps and small vases in red ceramic.

Port El Kantaoui

Port El Kantaoui is a gleaming white

purpose-built 'garden port' which focusses around an elegant marina. Probably it will set the pattern for future development along Tunisia's holiday coastlines. Located 4 miles north of central Sousse, and 15 miles from Monastir airport, its architectural style resembles that of Sidi Bou Said, just outside Tunis.

Building of the 800-acre project started in 1979, with initial finance mainly from Abou Dhabi. Today, two-thirds of the funding comes from Tunisia, and only the remaining one-third from the Gulf. Before the project got under way, lengthy studies were made. These highlighted the problem that, when Tunisian tourism started, it was based entirely on sun-and-sand holidays which cannot fully occupy hotels and staff for more than a limited period. There was a need to develop a high-category style of tourism - something that would attract visitors outside the peak sun-and-sand season.

Hence the idea of developing an integrated resort where visitors can find year-round activities: a pleasure centre based on the 340-berth Marina; golf; and a wide variety of other sport facilities. Around these basics, three types of accommodation are offered: a dozen hotels; 800 or more apartments with roof-top patios, for sale or rental; and an area where people can buy individual plots for construction of their own villas amid the jasmine bushes and olive trees. Two of the 4-star hotels get luxury rating, including the Hannibal Palace operated by Trust Houses Forte.

Surrounding the Marina is a self-contained village, with cobbled lanes lined with boutiques, super-market, police station, post office, bank, pharmacy, cafés, bars, restaurants and night club. The golf course has been extended to 27 holes, and the project is to build another extension to bring it up to 36.

Monastir

Mileage from Monastir: Tunis 100; Hammamet/Nabeul 70; Sousse 12; Gabès 150; Mahdia 30; Sfax 95; Tozeur 170.

Fine sandy beaches and cliffs along several miles of coastline are the setting for the holiday hotels of Monastir and Skanès-Plage. The Tourist Zone of Skanès-Plage is separated from the rest of Tunisia by a highway and several miles of salt pans. Typical of the top-grade hotels is the Kuriat Palace, located close to the airport and the Presidential Palace, amid gardens of palm, geranium and jasmine. With an all-marble entrance lobby, the Kuriat Palace is rated 4-star. Seven more hotels have a similar rating, while another half-dozen are 3-star including the 2100-bed Sahara Beach. Close neighbour of the Sahara Beach is Club Méditerranée. Between them, the resort hotels feature all the required sport and entertainment facilities, and there's an 18-hole course for the golfers.

Quite small in comparison with neighbouring Sousse, Monastir has been largely rebuilt in recent decades. The old Chraga central district has been totally revamped, and the town has a newly-built railway station, an international-grade conference centre, university buildings and a 20,000-seat sport stadium. As the birthplace of former President Bourguiba, Monastir has seen the building of a Presidential Palace for summer use, a glittering Bourguiba Mosque and a Bourguiba family mausoleum. Light industries have been established, while the airport, the new Metro (a suburban rail link with Sousse and Mahdia) and the numerous hotels and a catering school have all brought prosperity to the town.

At the Marina Cap Monastir is a smaller-scale version of the Port El Kantaoui complex, with luxurious air-conditioned apartments, a 400-berth harbour, beach, tennis courts, swimming-pool, cinema, night club, boutiques and restaurants. It's an attractive little Marina, very clean, with plenty of flowers. The project was financed by Arab money from the Gulf, and then was bought by the Tunisian government.

Quite close is Monastir's oldest monument: the Ribat, founded in the year 796 for the warrior monks who dedicated their lives to the defence of Islam against Christian attack. From the 11th century, Monastir was rated as a Holy City which contained a gate to Heaven. According to legend, a three-day stay in the Ribat gave pilgrims the right of entry into Paradise.

The massive castle walls and battlements are well preserved, and often appear in movies, and as a setting for summertime Sound and Light performances. Today the Ribat houses a Museum of the Islamic Arts - coins, manuscripts, Persian miniatures, pottery and glass. Greatest treasure of the museum is one of the world's oldest scientific instruments - an Arab-made astrolabe from the year 927.

Standing out with a pointed green tiled roof to its minaret, the Habib Bourguiba Mosque near the Ribat was erected in the ex-President's honour in 1966. Features have been borrowed from all periods of Tunisian architecture, with lavish use of multi-coloured stone, tilework and mosaics.

The prayer hall is supported by 86 columns of pink marble. Close by, the Bourguiba family mausoleum, with its gilded dome and twin towers, follows a similar elaborate style.

Opposite the Mosque entrance and next door to the Tourist Information Office is a charming little museum collection of traditional costumes. There's a good range of kaftans, wedding gowns and other male and female costume. Most of these traditional outfits look hot and heavy, as though designed for Alpine temperatures rather than North African. It's well worth a ten-minute look, or fifteen for the ladies. Entrance is free.

To find some more traditional workmanship, visit the large ONA handicraft store, almost next door. Noting their fixed prices, you'll then be better able to haggle in the private-sector shops.

Mahdia

Mahdia is not yet on the main tourist circuit. It has only two 3-star hotels, and around 1200 holidaymaker beds, but is well worth a daytime visit. The town is easily reached in 1½ hours from Monastir by train, bus or louage. Each form of transport terminates at the harbour, which ranks high among Tunisia's fishing ports, with a thriving local canning industry.

An open-sided concrete market, roofed over for cool shade, is location for fishermen tending their nets. A fruit and vegetable section offers splendid onions, new potatoes, peppers and fresh almonds. Alongside are the blue and white vessels of the Mahdia fishing fleet. Friday is Mahdia's market day, when the quayside becomes the focal point for a lively gathering of country folk and townspeople.

The main sightseeing attraction is the beautifully-preserved medina. You enter the enormously thick city walls through a passage called Skifa-bab Zouila, built by the Fatimides in the 10th century when they chose Mahdia to be their capital. The 'Dark Entrance', 48 yards long, was defended by several massive iron grills. Today, visitors are welcomed just opposite by an information office of the Syndicat d'Initiative. Just inside a gate to the right, brick steps lead up to the ramparts, with super views over the snow-white buildings of Mahdia, and round the golden-sand bay to where the holiday hotels are located.

Up the main street are sleepy shops of tourist interest - handicrafts, boutiques and jewelry, although Mahdia is not yet geared to holiday visitors in bulk. On the right is a Silk Museum. Further along, Place du Caire is a delightful little square with typical Tunisian low-profile buildings all around, and tea-house tables and chairs beneath the trees. Streets are clean and well swept. Plaster is peeling on private houses, but the general impression is of modest prosperity.

The Obeidite Mosque looks more like a castle, with solid walls and massive entrance gate. It's a renovated version of the 10th-century original. 'Entrance to the courtyard is forbidden to those whose clothing is not respectful.'

On the extreme tip of Cape Africa, restoration work has made a good job of the Castle (Borj el Kebir), which now looks impeccable. The building was enlarged by the Turks in 1595. An annual festival called Mahdia Nights is held from 25 July to end of August, with evening shows in the open courtyard: mainly folklore groups,

music and dance.

The direct coastal route between Monastir and Mahdia passes through a richly-cultivated area of olive groves and market gardens, with plastic greenhouses producing early vegetables and salad crops. Virtually every smallholding has an underground water reservoir, marked by its concrete lid. A salt lake called Moknine Sebkhet is surrounded by olive groves.

A whole-day circuit by rented car or public transport could be routed via El Djem. Catch an after-breakfast train from Sousse, arriving at El Djem an hour later. Spend two hours, to visit the Colosseum, the Museum, and the Roman villa excavations alongside. Then take a louage ride from the central square of El Djem to Mahdia, arriving within 40 minutes.

There's time for a leisurely fish lunch (at quite modest prices), and exploration of the Medina and the castle. You can then catch a train from Mahdia to Monastir and back to Sousse; or sample another louage, or the bus service.

The Mahdia-Monastir train journey is delightful. You can travel first class air-conditioned quite cheaply, sitting on the shady right-hand side of the carriage, with good views of the sea coast.

Sfax

Sfax is Tunisia's largest industrial town, and second in population. Industries include olive-oil processing, and the export of other agricultural products, salt and phosphates. Frankly there's not much room for tourism amid this bustling prosperity, and it's not usually more than a meal or refreshment stop on sightseeing tours. A few charter flights arrive at Sfax airport, particularly for holidays on the Kerkennah Islands.

The approach to Sfax by road from resorts to the north is usually by highway GP 1 through a somewhat featureless landscape with parched earth, huge plantations of olive trees, almonds and apricots, and occasional grazing flocks of sheep. Many fields are hedged with prickly pear. For most of the road between El Djem and Sfax you can quite cheerfully go to sleep without missing anything much.

The regimental lines of olives were mainly established by French colonizers, though the land has now been returned to the Tunisians who continue with the more scientific widely-spaced planting of the trees to encourage a good spread of the root systems. Harvesting is from November, when workers strip the branches with fingers protected by curved ram's-horns - or, today, the same shape in tough plastic. Only dripping blood and a frightened redhead are missing from a clutching-hand effect normal on thriller book-jackets. An average tree produces a hundredweight of olives, yielding just over three gallons of oil.

In general, there's not too much to grab holidaymaker interest in the modern town of Sfax, rebuilt since heavy bombing during the North African campaigns. However, the medina is well worth an hour or two: turretted city walls to admire, interesting features around the Great Mosque, and a folk museum at Dar Djellouli, a graceful palace built 1728.

The lively inner harbour shelters a wide range of craft which specialise in sponge-diving, catching octopus, and fishing with the help of palm-frond traps - as seen on the Kerkennah Islands and around Djerba. At the port, people cluster for an informal market. Hucksters make their pitch from the tailgate of small vans.

The Kerkennah Islands

For peace and quiet on a desert island, go to the Kerkennah Islands. This escapist's paradise is located 18 miles offshore from Sfax. The one-hour crossing by ferry costs 35p. As you approach the first of the low-lying islands, it looks as though scattered palm trees are growing out of the sea. Closer, and the island takes shape, more like a low-lying sandspit.

At El Kantara, a Roman causeway links the two main islands, Chergui and Gharbi. There's the archetypal view of brilliantly blue sea, a line of yellow sand, and wind-blown palm trees silhouetted against the skyline. A couple of two-star hotels and a holiday village are grouped in the tourist area of Sidi Farej, 12 miles from the ferry landing.

Along most of the Kerkennah coast, the sea is ideal for children, very shallow and sandy. Catering for the bucket-and-spade clientele, the Grand Hotel operates a Kiddies Club. Among suggestions on the weekly programme are painting competitions, sand-castle contests, a children's fancy dress party, shell collecting on the beach, a kiddies disco, and a treasure hunt. There is children's video every morning at 11 a.m., and adults' video at 9.30 each evening.

The Grand Hotel also has a resident camel, who charges 2 dinars per half-hour trip. Among other means of transport, there are bicycles and boats for hire, and windsurfers are available. Frankly speaking, few people go to the Kerkennah Islands for the shopping or the nightlife. In the hotel boutique you can buy T-shirts with palm-trees on them; and there's a chemist's at Ramla, the capital. For nightlife, pack some good books. Otherwise there are no temptations to pull you away from basking on the beach, or around the hotel pool.

Kerkennah is light on sightseeing. A half-day mini-bus circuit covers the lot. A stop could be made at Ramla, where there's a carpet factory, though it's not a sales outlet. Straight on there are salt flats, which usually have a mirage or two. The fishing harbour of El Ataia specialises in catching octopus and in building boats.

Crucial to the octopus hunt are earthenware jars which are wide at the top, narrowing down in the classic shape of Greek amphorae. These pots are strung on lines, and lowered into the water at 10-yard intervals. The octopus appreciate these prefabricated caves, and move in. Later, the fishermen pull up the pots, remove any squatters, and lower away to attract a new tenant. The octopus are hung up to dry on washing lines, and then find a ready export market to Japan and other gourmet countries.

This style of octopus pot is common elsewhere in Tunisia. Catches are good in this shallow tidal sea, rich in seafood. The hotels can even offer octopus salad on the set menu - something of a delicacy, remarkable for a two-star hotel. Squid and prawns are likewise prolific.

For another ususual style of fishing, all around the coastline you'll see what look like wattle fences, made of palm fronds, reaching out to sea from the beaches. From the holiday hotels, you can easily paddle out to inspect them closer. Fish come in-shore with the tide. When they swim parallel to the beach they find their way blocked by the fencing.

Their reaction is to avoid the obstacle by swimming out to sea. But the end of the fence is shaped like an arrowhead which funnels them to the tip. That's the end of the road, with netting. They swim through what looks like a hole in the net, but it leads into a cage with no escape route. These cages like big lobster-pots range from about 2 feet in diameter up to 6 feet. Once or twice a day, they are hauled in. A similar system operates around the island of Djerba.

Back to the boatyard at El Ataia: skills are traditional, and the preferred material is wood. Much of the timber is imported from places like Sweden, although some local olive wood is used. The industry is fostered by Government support, backed by Italian aid.

A few miles round the coast is a modest museum which commemorates Habib Bourguiba's escape to Libya in 1945, when he was in trouble with the French because of his political struggle for independence.

The boat in which Tunisia's future President took flight is sheltered by a simple roof. It's a flat-bottomed boat - locally called a *loud* - specially evolved for use around the shallow waters of the Kerkennah Islands. The small museum contains a number of Bourguiba's letters, written in Arabic, in which he appealed for international help in his struggle against the French. This seems to be Kerkennah's greatest claim for a paragraph in history, apart from the odd little fact that rejects from the Bey's harem were exiled here.

Transport

Since 1986 a Metro train has operated between Sousse and Monastir, serving the airport and the main hotels of Skanès Plage. It runs at about one-hourly intervals, and costs roughly 35p first class for the half-hour journey. Departure from Sousse is at a corner of the harbour, by Bab Djedid and the fish market. From Monastir station, a connecting coastal link goes through to Mahdia.

If you want to use long-distance bus services, check at the hotel or the Tourist Information Office on timings, and from where they start.

To Kairouan, get the bus from Bab Djedid – that's the nearest city gate to the fish market by the port. It's a 1½-hour journey costing £1, with five departures daily. Most of the shared-taxi louage services start from this location opposite the Metro station. Signs are posted to indicate destinations. At first sight it all looks chaotic, but passengers are rapidly sorted into the right vehicles, with minimal waiting-time.

Buses to Mahdia go from Place du Port - a 2-hour journey costing £1 - 12 departures daily.

To Hammamet and Nabeul, there are two departures a day - taking about 2 hours for £1.30.

Numerous local buses - including a low-cost ride to Port El Kantaoui - start from Sidi Yahia by the city ramparts, behind the Syndicat d'Initiative.

Le Petit Train is something of a transport joke, which started operating in 1987. It is hugely successful, considering that it charges much more than the regular bus. For two persons, taxis are cheaper. Blue and white open trolleys are towed along the road by a Noddy-type engine, which emits suitable sound effects like a train whistle. Sometimes Le Petit Train tops up its fuel tank at a petrol filling station. It goes from the Boujaffar Promenade in Sousse to Port el Kantaoui, following the tourist route to the Marina. There are request stops at a number of hotels along the way: El Hanna Beach, Riadh, Jawhara, Marabout, Marhaba, Tour Khalef, Ulysse, Salem, Shehrazade. Often it starts full, so that people waiting en route are left standing.

More serious trains can reach Tunis in 2 hours, or go south to El Djem, Sfax, Tozeur and Gabès. Timings of trains change, following a seasonal pattern. Trains are smartly decorated in the standard livery of white, blue and yellow - a theme which is picked out also in the railway station.

Daily sea trips are operated by the 'El Mahjoubi' - mostly morning or afternoon circuits that last 3½ hours, or whole-day trips, which can include the chance of fishing. The circuits link Sousse, Port el Kantaoui and the Kuriate Islands opposite Monastir. Two other boats do similar trips: the 'Mabourka' and the 'Aziza'.

Excursions

The experience of Tunisia gives you the chance of returning with memories that will last longer than just a suntan and a new pair of sandals. Within a 60-mile radius of the Sousse-Monastir resorts is good choice of half-day or whole-day excursions, particularly to Kairouan for sightseeing of the Islamic holy city and carpet-weaving centre; to El Djem for its Colosseum, the finest Roman monument in Africa; or to Hammamet and Nabeul, on Friday for the popular market at Nabeul.

Spreading the net further, a one-day trip to Tunis is memorable for the shopping potential of the souks - like the medina of Sousse, but much more extensive - and for the Roman mosaics of the Bardo Museum. Certainly worth seeing, if your appetite has been whetted by the mosaics in the museum at the Sousse Kasbah! A tightly-packed day can also include a visit to what's left of Carthage, with time to wander through the idyllic village of Sidi Bou Said.

Looking south, a fast-paced one-day safari includes El Djem, the maritime oasis of Gabès with time for a carriage ride, and a look at the incredible cave dwellings of Matmata. On a two-day or three-day circuit, the inland oases such as Douz, Tozeur and Nefta could also feature in the itinerary.

Finally there is choice of one-day excursions to other Roman sites of the interior, with Dougga as the highspot.

Nightlife

Nightlife centres mainly on the individual hotels. Your tour-operator rep can advise where is the action each evening at neighbouring hotels. Here are some to sample, but check first on the local scene: El Hanna Disco; Club 80, under El Hanna Beach, with drinks expensive; La Grotte, in grounds of Tour Khalef; and Marhaba Night Club.

These night clubs generally open around 9 p.m., and often have a floor show at around 11 p.m. An entrance fee of about £1 is normally charged for non-residents of the hotels. Drinks are always higher-priced than in the hotel bars.

There are three folklore centres in the Sousse area. One is called Loukala, in the Medina. Another is El Bourg at

Sidi Bou Ali, a village about 12 miles from Sousse on the highway north towards Tunis. A third rival is Bellaoum at the village of Kalaa Kebira, about 25 minutes' drive from Sousse. Visits are organised through travel agencies.

Dining out

Outside the à la carte restaurants in main hotels, Sousse offers over 30 tourist-grade restaurants. A short list includes the following:

Le Lido, Avenue Mohammed V, facing Sousse harbour - mainly Tunisian dishes, and good sea-food.

L'Escargot, Route de la Corniche - French cuisine.

Les Sportifs, Avenue Bourguiba - Tunisian, cheap but good.

La Marmite, rue Rémada - Tunisian, reasonably priced.

L'Olivier, rue Mongi Slim - for meat dishes.

Hong-Kong, Boulevard de Rabat -Chinese.

L'Albatros, Route de la Corniche - pizzas.

Régal, Boulevard Abdelhamid El Kadhi - cosmopolitan.

Flouka, rue du 2 Mars 1934, opposite Magasin Modern - approximately Italian cuisine, reasonably priced.

At Port el Kantaoui there are several good but pricey restaurants. Best is **l'Escale**, which ranks as top-grade international; and **les Emirs** - excellent menu choice, with gourmet specialty of lamb cooked in an earthenware pot.

At Monastir: **Hotel Yasmine**, run by an Englishwoman.

6. Djerba – Island of the Lotus Eaters

Mileage to Djerba: Tunis 320; Hammamet/Nabeul 290; Sousse 220; Sfax 160; Gabès 80; Gafsa 230; Tozeur 220.

Odysseus came to the Island of the Lotus Eaters by ship. The Romans built a causeway from the mainland, so they could march across. Today's visitors arrive mostly by air charter. Otherwise, relatively little has changed over the past 3,000 years. If you want to be a modern-day lotus-eater, even just for a fortnight, Djerba offers retreat from the go-getting life-style. Whatever may be the secret of the lotus, it can be the staff of life during a Djerba holiday.

According to Homer, Odysseus made a Djerba stopover when a Force Nine gale drove him off course during his Mediterranean cruise. He sent three crew members ashore to get fresh water. Hospitable natives offered them lotus - a fruit which gave eaters a complete distaste for active life, and a preference for indolent, luxurious enjoyment. Tired of roaming, they wanted to stay. Odysseus had to use firm measures to stop the rot. He clapped the would-be deserters in irons and sailed away with them, deaf to their protests at being yanked back to the world of work and worries.

Ever since Homer sang this beguiling story, botanists have eagerly tried to identify the lotus. Typical poet, Homer was short on hard facts. He merely described the lotus as 'the honeyed fruit of the plant'. Later writers tried to fill in some descriptive details, mainly by guesswork. An expanded text says: 'The lotus is a thorny wild shrub, giving a fruit the size of an olive, which in growing turns purple. The taste is between the date and the fig, with a pleasant smell. A delicious drink is extracted which has the flavour of wine.'

The nearest plant which partly answers to that description is the jujube tree, with a small plum-like fruit ripening to a reddish brown. Gathered in September, it is preserved by storage. Gradually the pulp becomes softer and sweeter than when fresh, and is valued in the Mediterranean as a dessert. The only drawback is that there are no jujube trees currently on Djerba.

However, in the holiday market, lotus-eating is precisely the image which copy-writers want to promote. Djerba has a head start, as a dreamy holiday island where modern man can relax. Go-getters over the centuries have been absorbed into the rhythm of life in a land where clocks have stood still for 2,000 years. Part of Djerba's appeal is to see reminders of those ancient civilizations.

Descendants of one of the world's oldest Jewish colonies still specialise in jewelry designs that were fashionable when Nebuchadnezzar was king of Babylon. The Roman causeway to the

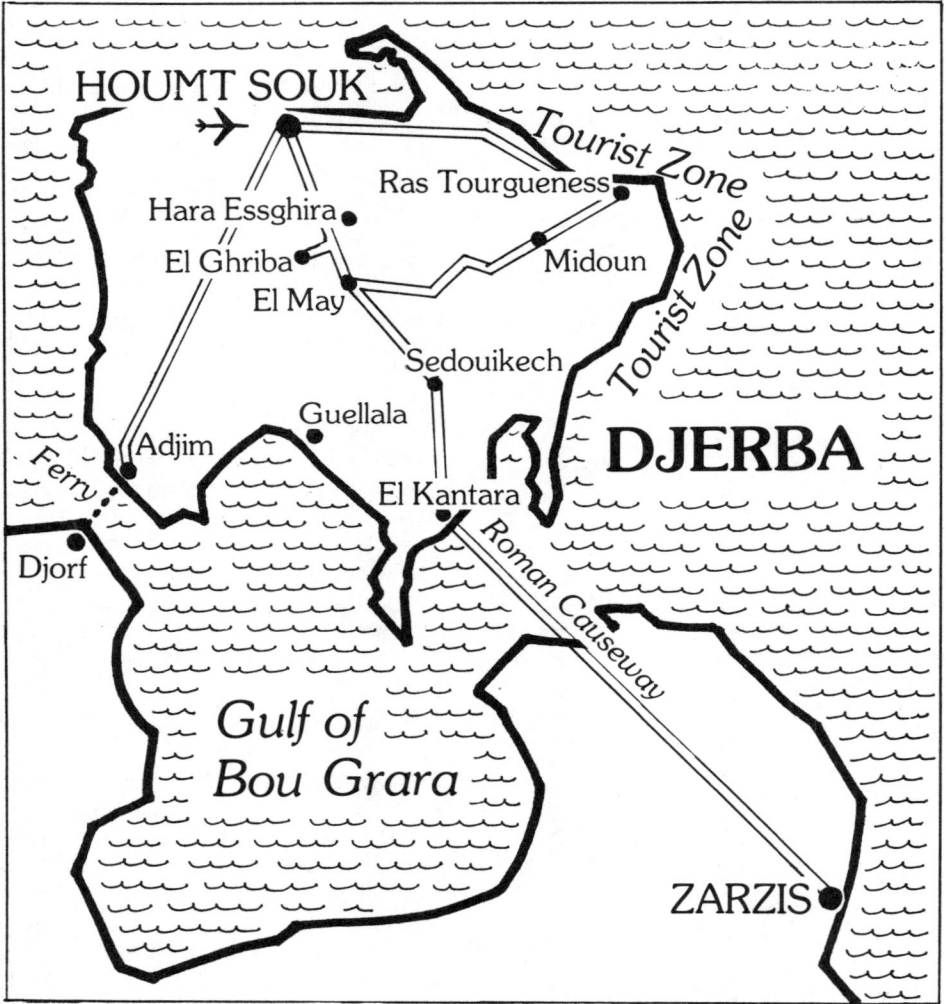

HOUMT SOUK

Ras Tourgueness

Hara Essghira

El Ghriba

El May

Midoun

Sedouikech

Guellala

DJERBA

Ferry

Adjim

El Kantara

Tourist Zone

Tourist Zone

Roman Causeway

Djorf

*Gulf of
Bou Grara*

ZARZIS

mainland carries road traffic to the seaside oasis of Zarzis on the mainland, where a spin-off holiday resort flourishes. Potters at Guellala use ancient Greek techniques unchanged since their wheels first began to spin two or three thousand years ago. Despite varied invasions, Djerban culture and language have remained basically Berber. They were there when the Phoenicians landed and set up a purple-cloth industry based on extracting dye from a local mussel called murex. The Phoenician and Roman town of Meninx has crumbled away, but traditional cloth-weaving continues at Sedouikech close by.

The waters around Djerba are mostly shallow, though somewhat deeper on the east coast. Normally you must go a mile or two out to sea before the depth reaches 15 feet. Unusually for the Mediterranean, the waters are tidal. Like an oasis-island extension of the Sahara Desert, Djerba enjoys 340 days of sunny skies. Beaches are magnificent. The highest point of Djerba - 18 miles broad by 14 - is only 182 feet above sand-dune level.

In contrast to arid stretches of the mainland, Djerba offers a more friendly landscape, with pleasant farmhouses dotted between olive plantations. Despite the lotus-eating tradition, the 20th century has begun to arrive. Djerba is reasonably prosperous.

Children ride bicycles, teenagers weave around on mopeds, adults have full-power motor-bikes, and village women return home sedately from market by shared taxi. Donkey carts are still around, but used mainly by dozy octagenarians. Camels now work almost entirely in tourism, though a few farmers still keep a resident camel for ploughing or for working the irrigation system. Otherwise, for general transport, the camel is old technology.

In the history of the island, the various settlers, conquerors and transient invaders - Phoenicians, Carthaginians, Romans, Byzantines, Arabs, Normans, Spaniards, Turks and French - have left very small mark on Djerba. Even when the Arabs arrived with the doctrine of Islam, it was the Arabs who were Berberized, rather than vice versa, and the Djerbans have chosen to follow the separatist Moslem creed of Kharijism.

In the last quarter-century, the new religion of topless sun-worship has been confined to the Tourist Zone of sandy beaches along the north-eastern coast, while Djerbans continue to swathe themselves head to foot in sheets or blankets, crowned by a sombrero when venturing into the sun.

In former times, little habitation existed along this section of coast. There was no question of tourism taking over a fishing village, and then swamping it in Costa Brava style. When the tourism industry started to build beach holiday complexes, nobody was displaced. This follows the pattern of Djerban history.

Long-term, Djerba's inhabitants have followed an in-depth defence policy of settling away from the coast in self-preservation from pirates and foreign invaders. The characteristic Djerban dwelling is a farmhouse stronghold built well inland. There are no hills to fortify.

Typically, three inland villages - the market centre of Midoun, and Mahboubine and El May, which feature two of Djerba's most magnificent mosques - surround a region of orchards, which depend on an underground freshwater table. The inhabitants live in *menzels* - domed farmhouses, greatly enlarged as extended families grow by marriages or births. Mostly the houses are spacious, well maintained with dazzling whitewash that gleams in the sun. Some have pleasant terraces, decorative grillwork, and glazed ceramics on the outside walls.

Houses are well separated, to preserve privacy, and are generally located on land cultivated by the head of the household, for whom farming is either a primary or a secondary occupation. The houses - with their domed rooves and small apertures - are designed for defence against attack, and against the heat. Rainwater reservoirs indicate the constant effort to offset water shortage.

Many storerooms are semi-underground. It's easier to dig a pit and cover it with a barrel-vaulted roof, rather than to find building materials to construct entirely above ground. Field boundaries are marked by earth banks, topped by cactus, prickly pear or palm fronds. Small herds of sheep and black goats dot the landscape.

Most of the land on Djerba can be cultivated, with crops of wheat, barley, fruit and vegetables. There are nearly 600,000 olive trees and 200,000 palm trees. Because of proximity to the sea, the dates are poor quality. But the figs, apples, apricots and pomegranates are good.

Holiday Hotels

From the airport, a ring road by-passes Houmt Souk, and follows a Route Touristique - marked by a yellow road sign - to the northeast corner of the island. At each crossroads, all the principal hotels of the tourist zone are signposted.

Around 20 low-profile establishments are spread along 12 blissful miles of excellent sand, with palm-groves and undeveloped coastline in between. Sand-yachting is possible where dead-flat sands are swept by good winds. Near the corner lighthouse at Cape Tourgueness, a long inlet of the sea greatly extends the area of beach. Each hotel or holiday village is a self-contained mini-resort, offering everything from ping-pong to beauty salons. Close to each hotel, tourist-industry camels, horses and carriages queue for customers. Nights are animated with folklore and belly-dancers. A Festival of Ulysses - mainly folklore routines - is held annually in high summer.

Four hotels rate four stars; another three have three-star status; the rest are mostly two-star. Biggest of all is the Dar Jerba, a huge 2400-bed complex operated like a Butlin's in four languages - French, German, English and Italian. Club Med runs two villages with almost 1000 capacity each. Pioneer among the hotels is the Aljazira, located 7 miles from Houmt Souk. Among its attractions is a thermal swimming pool, laced with iron and sulphur. Close by is the entertainment and leisure centre of Aljazira, which opened in 1981.

Among the captive poets who write hotel brochures, the accolade must go to the Tanit Hotel's wordsmith: 'On a sandy infinity interrupted by myriads of palms and olive-trees in a symphony of ochre and green cameo on sea-background, Jerba, the island of softness and forgetting, shelters in a honey-yellow purse the splendid Tanit.'

66

Like Odysseus' crew members, few lotus-hooked holidaymakers will want to leave that kind of setting. However, a regular bus service into Houmt Souk goes past all the hotels, roughly at 45-minute intervals, though Djerban bus-drivers are innoculated against Germanic clock-watching. The easiest contact with traditional Djerba is in the market centres. Visitors are welcome with their cameras and dinars to photograph the local life and buy souvenirs.

Best places to visit are Houmt Souk particularly on market days of Monday and Thursday, Midoun for its Friday market, Guellala for pottery, and Sedouikech for basket work, straw hats, hampers and woven rush mats. There are half-day island tours by coach, or shopping trips with guide. Otherwise, bicycle hire makes sense for exploring the pancake-flat island.

The slower you travel, the better chance of enjoying all the country scenes, the costumes of country folk, and vignettes of farming life. Sheep and goats are watched by herdsmen who lounge in the shade of palm trees. Donkeys are tethered to a hitching post or to an olive tree. Schoolgirls run along with their satchels, black pony-tails a-swinging in the wind.

For longer journeys, it's easy to book sightseeing trips to the mainland. One-day and two-day coach or Land Rover excursions go to Gabès and Matmata; to the oases of Kebili and Douz, or to Tozeur and Nefta; up the coast to Sousse and Kairouan; or south to the ksar territory of Tataouine and Chenini. You can even do Tozeur and Nefta by air and motor coach.

Houmt Souk

Houmt Souk - meaning 'Market Centre' - is the capital of Djerba, which is twice the size of Malta. With its port and commerce, Houmt Souk is Djerba's most important town, absorbing one-third of the island's 100,000 population. Houmt Souk is small enough to drift around in an hour or two, without much risk of getting lost. As you wander, you'll come across the main sightseeing highlights.

From the central square called Place Bechir Seoud, most visitors gravitate towards the souks. These ancient covered alleys are lined with tiny open-fronted shops. All the typical craftware is on show: woollen blankets, engraved jewelry, copper and leather items. Hard bargaining is essential, as all the merchants are wide awake when there's prospect of a sale.

Reputed as shrewd traders, Djerbans have a tradition of opening grocery stores on the mainland, and later retiring to Djerba on the profits. Go to Houmt Souk on a market day - Monday or Thursday - when the town is at its liveliest, crammed with local colour. In the fish market, the day's catch is sold by auction. Sometimes black musicians come to town, adding to the frenzy.

There are 213 mosques in Djerba, but Houmt Souk can easily fill your requirement for photos of dazzling white minarets, sharply silhouetted against the blue sky. Most picturesque is the Turkish Mosque (Djama Tourk), rivalled by the more elaborate Strangers' Mosque. Opposite Strangers' Mosque is a triangular square where taxis are lined up outside a *hammam* - Turkish-type bath - and the 17th-century semi-fortress of the Zaouia Sidi Brahim, a religious teaching establishment which also gave accommodation for travellers. You can peep into the courtyard, but cannot go much further.

By the seashore is Borj el Kébir, a former Spanish fort built 1289 on a Roman site. In 1507 it became a stronghold of Turkish privateers, which is a polite word for pirates. A joint expedition of Papal forces with the Knights of Malta sailed in 1560 to clear out the Turks, but the result was total disaster. Hundreds - possibly thousands - of Christian skulls were piled in a gruesome tower on the beach, about 100 yards from the fortress as you walk towards the fishing harbour. A plaque marks the spot.

In another direction from the main town - westwards, towards the Sidi Mahrez beach - is a small Regional Museum in a charming building which needs external repair. It features popular arts and traditions - costumes, marriage chests, Jewish and Berber jewelry, ancient pottery and household utensils. Par for the course is 15 minutes. Closed on Friday.

Back around the central squares are plentiful cafés and restaurants. There's the usual Café Sportif, where the main sport is dominoes.

Among the tourist restaurants of Houmt Souk, here's an approximate order of merit: the Princesse d'Haroun, Tebsi, Méditerranée, Blue Moon, Baccar, de l'Isle, Restaurant du Sud, El Hana, Neptun, Tebsi. They are tightly grouped together by the souks, so it's easy to make comparison shopping of their menus before deciding which to choose. Prices are very moderate. In the middle price-range there's choice of plat du jour - spaghetti, or chicken or tajine - for just over a pound. A fish couscous, or a lamb couscous costs £2; a Royal Couscous - served with three different types of meat - is around £2.50.

For a memorable fish dinner, choose the Princesse d'Haroun Restaurant, just by the port. It has 200 seats upstairs, and can seat 500 below and outdoors. A Tunisian band entertains, with a belly-dancer to oscillate several times every evening. The waiters are dressed casual, each with a jasmine flower tucked behind his ear.

Midoun

Midoun is a merchants' village, where each street has its speciality. There's a section for grain and spice merchants, another for butchers, yet another for fruit and veg. Easily reached from the Tourist Zone hotels, Midoun is best on market day, held every Friday. Midoun is then crowded with local farmers, and it's easy to capture pictures of traditional costume while you pretend to focus on a pile of onions.

Farmers display their produce on mats along the roadway. Nuts, beans and varied spices are weighed out in scoops from open sacks. Across the road are regular and tourist shops crammed with handicrafts. Half a street is brilliant with carpets, hung from balconies. Further along, it's all brassware and bangles.

Tourists and locals buy straw hats, especially the conical-shaped sombrero called *midhalla*, which has been high fashion in Berber villages for 2000-odd years. It's the same design as the ancient Greek hat called *petasos*. If you miss market day at Midoun, you can still catch the same atmosphere elsewhere: Sedouikech Tuesday; Ajim Sunday; Guellala Wednesday.

Guellala

Guellala is the potters' village at the southern end of the island. They use red or yellow clay from nearby hills to fashion unglazed amphorae, household water pots, jars and mugs that are sold throughout North Africa. Well established in Carthaginian and Roman times, they produced the Ali Baba jars in which olive oil was shipped to Carthage and later to Rome. Occasionally you see men striding into the sea, loading great pottery jars aboard small sailing boats which await thirty yards off-shore. But most export deliveries today are by truck.

In recent decades, tourism has changed the standard production line. Down the central street, virtually every workshop has switched to the glazed ware which customers prefer: ashtrays, vases copied from old designs, candlesticks, plates, coffee cups and saucers. Potters who respect tradition will recommend these objects in unglazed terracotta. You may find them more attractive than when glazed, but they are also more fragile. You can ask a potter to throw an object of your own design, which he'll do while you watch. But then you have to return another day to pick it up.

Adjim

If you approach Djerba from the mainland direction of Gabès - through the Mareth Line, where Italian and German forces were defeated by the Eighth Army during the North African campaign of 1943 - the easiest access is by regular ferry from Djorf to Adjim. Carrying between 12 and 16 vehicles, two ferries shuttle at half-hour intervals throughout the day, with occasional crossings even during the small hours.

Sheep, camels and donkeys are also carried, though the ship of the desert doesn't take kindly to water, and can easily get seasick. However, once aboard and kneeling down tidily, a camel will accept his fate with dignity, merely baring his yellow teeth in disdain for such an unnatural form of transport.

Here is the narrowest point across the water, where a corner of Djerba comes within two miles of the South Tunisian coast. North and westwards is the broad sweep of the Gulf of Gabès; south and east is the almost entirely enclosed Gulf of Bou Grara. Like a shallow lagoon, Bou Grara teems with seafood. Lateen-rigged fishing vessels ripple serenely into harbour, but a few decorative shipwrecks remind the traveller that these very shallow waters can have their dangers, especially when sudden squalls blow up. Just off-shore are fish traps like those at the Kerkennah Islands.

Adjim is clean and prosperous-looking, with gleaming-white colonnades and at least ten mosques. The little town is the second fishing port after Houmt Souk, but its principal activity is sponge diving. Sponges are cleaned in Adjim, cellophane-wrapped and sold at the Office des Pêches or in shops at a fixed price. Real sponges have become a luxury, so seize the opportunity!

A Djerban hint: hang a sponge by a nylon thread from your bathroom ceiling. Soak a few lentils for a couple of days. Then put one into each of the sponge's cells and spray them now and then. After about a fortnight your sponge will be transformed into a decorative ball of greenery.

The Roman causeway

The Romans were foot-soldiers rather

than sailors. So, appropriately, they had the original idea of linking Djerba to the mainland by a causeway. The line they chose was near to an arm of Djerba that reaches from present-day El Kantara towards the mainland. Their causeway was four miles long, built of submerged blocks that acted like the wall of a dam across the eastern entrance to the almost-enclosed Gulf of Bou Grara, which the Romans called Lake Triton. A road then led off from the island towards Libya and Tripoli.

When the Romans left Tunisia in the 5th century, the causeway fell into disrepair. The Tarik-el-Jemil - Road of the Camel - could only be crossed at low tide in the fifteen following centuries by sure-footed camels led by a knowledgeable guide who waded ahead. Even then, midway across, there was a major break in the submerged causeway, reputedly cut in 1551 by pirates to provide a bolt-hole from the Gulf, when they were hard pressed by a Genoese fleet.

Meanwhile, Djerban life continued on its placid course, with local fishermen earning a steady living over the centuries. Then, in the early 1950's, French engineers surveyed the line of the causeway with the intention of linking Djerba to the mainland by a modern highway for motor traffic. Using the original Roman foundations, the causeway was raised to several feet above the normal sea level, and the former facility was restored after an interval of 1500 years.

Apart from complaints from the fishermen, who could now enter and leave the Gulf only by the single neck at Adjim on the west, the new road was a boon for heavier lorry and bus traffic which was too heavy for the former lightweight car ferry of Adjim.

After several more years, the fishermen's complaints became louder. Since far-off times, fishing in the Gulf had always been rich and dependable. Now, they claimed, their catches were steadily dwindling. They blamed the new causeway. Fishery experts came to study the problem. Their verdict supported the local fishermen. Formerly, they reported, fish had migrated through the eastern entrance to spawn in the shallow Gulf. Then, with the rebuilt causeway sealing off the entrance, they had gone elsewhere.

The solution was simple: to cut a gap in the causeway, half-way across, so that the egg-laying shoals could pass through. Today the situation is restored. Fish stocks have returned to normal. Vessels lower their masts and pass beneath a road bridge. Engineering, science and general know-how has been vindicated. How clever we are, in the 20th century!

Curiously, the former theory that pirates had cut through the Roman causeway is no longer accepted. Instead, it's now realised that the Romans deliberately built their causeway with a gap half-way across, protected by a drawbridge and a guard-post. That may have been purely for defense. But, more likely, Roman civil engineers had grasped the fish-spawning problem 2000 years ago.

The Jewish villages

A fascinating survival is one of the world's oldest Jewish communities, which sought refuge from Babylonian captivity in 585 BC, when Nebuchadnezzar was king. This exodus was followed by another from Jerusalem in 71 BC. Closely grouped in two villages called Hara Kebira and Hara Seghira - Big Ghetto and Little

Ghetto - the colony kept its traditions intact, like a chapter from the Old Testament.

In more recent times, many of the Jewish population have departed, mostly to Israel, though there was never any anti-Jewish movement in Tunisia. An estimated 1500 Jews still remain. That figure is elastic, depending whom you ask. On departure, most of the Jewish houses were sold, but some were retained by their owners who occasionally return for a holiday. The twin villages have been renamed Essouani and Erryadh.

Focal point of the community is El Ghriba - 'the Marvellous' - claimed to be one of the world's oldest synagogues in continued occupation. Founded when the community first settled 2500 years ago, El Ghriba is a place of pilgrimage visited especially on the 33rd day of Passover by Jews from elsewhere in Tunisia, but also from many other countries, including USA, France and Israel itself.

In fact, the present building is a rebuilt 1920 version, replacing the original which burnt down. Walls are covered with tiles, and the general appearance is ornate. But it's the authentic site of one of Judaism's most ancient places of worship. Pride of the community is a collection of Torahs. A caretaker shows visitors to an inner sanctum, unlocks a carved wooden cupboard, and displays a splendid ceremonial Torah - a great parchment scroll set in a cylindrical case of heavily chased silver and sandalwood. A donation is expected, like half a dinar. Heads must be covered, and shoes removed.

Attached to the synagogue is a large hostel which can accommodate several hundred pilgrims. Rooms are ranged around a courtyard, with a gleaming whitewashed balcony going around the upper floor. There's a separate room for each family, and communal kitchens.

The remaining Jewish villagers wear virtually the same costume as their Moslem neighbours, though their head-dress is different. Their houses often carry the Jewish seven-branched candlestick symbol, or a fish design, by the entrance. Some Jewish families live closer to Houmt Souk, and carry on a tradition of jewelry craftsmanship. They produce delicate work in gold and enamel, specializing in designs that were fashionable when their forefathers left Jerusalem in 70 BC - or even in the earlier exodus of 585 BC.

Zarzis

As a beach resort, Zarzis is like an offspring of Djerba, linked by the umbilical cord of the Roman causeway from El Kantara. The nearest arrival airport is 32 miles away, on Djerba. Long beaches of fine golden sand face north-east onto the open Mediterranean. Twelve miles south is Lake Bibane, a lagoon, rich in fish.

From the shoreline of the Gulf of Bou Grara, an oasis stretches nine miles into the town of Zarzis. Three small villages and a few scattered houses blend in with the countryside. The oasis has half a million palm trees, and about 150,000 olive trees. Citrus and early vegetables such as asparagus are grown, though yields are poor because of high salt content in the artesian well water. Eucalyptus and acacias help check erosion, and some areas are terraced.

The main cash crop is the olive, which has thrived since Roman times. The oil was shipped to Rome, mainly for lighting purposes. Engineers of 1700 years ago even built an 'oleoduct' from their city of Ziane, down to the port. Could this be the world's first oil pipeline?

More recent expansion of the olive groves came through a French project of the 1950's to settle families of the nomadic Accara Bedouin tribe, who successfully converted apparently arid desert into flourishing olive-tree plantations. The large olive harvest has promoted ancillary industries: oil extraction plants, both modern and antiquated, and soap manufacture.

Outside of the fabulous beaches, mainly served by five hotel or holiday village complexes - three of 3-star grade, and two 2-star - there's really not much else besides working on your suntan. Two hotels - Zita and Zarzis - feature hot-spring swimming pools, running at 79°F. Between them, the five hotels have room for over 3,500 guests. Their grounds are spacious enough to contain all entertainment, sport and camel-riding facilities within their garden perimeters. Nightlife beyond the hotels is zero. The principal outside restaurants are l'Olivier, Les Palmiers, Le Pacha and Abou Nawas.

Local sightseeing? After you've seen the first thousand olive trees, you can skip the remaining 149,000. There's a lively Friday market, which shouldn't be missed, especially as you'll see a good range of Bedouin costume. On other days, merchants sit around gossiping, or they meditate deeply with eyes closed. The harbour is a sponge-fishing base. Divers use long-handled tridents - same design as Neptune's - for stabbing and uprooting their quarry.

From Zarzis it's easy to visit highlights of the South on day trips. Otherwise, for more scenic variety, better go on any available excursions or bus-rides across the Roman causeway to the island of Djerba.

What to buy in Djerba

Woollen *foutas* - long pieces of beautiful white woollen fabric. The wool is spun and woven by hand. These materials wash very well; and the more you wash them the better.

Wool blankets - if you don't like the patterns or colours, you can order a colour or size of your choosing. Shopkeepers are often manufacturers as well. Make sure you are not leaving the next day!

Bedouin belts - these have been adapted to fit a European waist. (Bedouin women wear them on their hips). They are soft, and of bold colouring. They can also be used as curtain loops.

Travelling bags of camel hide or other leather - hard-wearing and well proportioned. The older they get, the shinier their finish.

Slippers from Tataouine - made out of embroidered leather in many colours.

Paintings - these are very simple, but many are quite charming in their innocence. They can be found at carpet stores or souvenir shops.

Klims - traditional rugs from Djerba. These are the cheapest rugs available.

Antiques - daggers, Berber and other antique jewelry, wooden chests, some inlaid with mother of pearl.

Pottery - buy your pottery in Guellala, where it is made.

Jewelry - wide choice of traditional ear-rings, 'Fatima's Hands', necklaces, and chunky silver bracelets called kholkahl, which are worn on Bedouin women's ankles.

72

7. The Great South – Oases, Desert and Cave-dwellers

Draw a line from Sfax to Gafsa, along Highway GP 14. Virtually everything that stretches west and south is an empty land of dramatic desert, with mountains, dried-up valleys and salt flats called Chotts. Human life centres around scattered oases and isolated wells, discovered and exploited over the centuries by men determined to conquer the wasteland. It's a lifestyle that is worlds apart from anything in northern Europe.

For a holidaymaker along Tunisia's coastline, a trip to the South - particularly to the golden triangle of Gabès, Tozeur and Matmata - adds a flavour of the Sahara to the Mediterranean package. On short excursions - anything from one to three days - it's easy to visit the highlights.

Deep south along the GP 19 road towards the Libyan Desert are the ksars - village fortress granaries - perched on rocky peaks with their strange constructions known as ghorfas. At Foum Tataouine on Monday market day, inhabitants of the surrounding Berber villages meet together: from Chenini, Douiret and Ghermassa, eagle's-nest locations which all have troglodyte dwellings dug into steep mountain slopes.

Touristic star of the South is Matmata, easily reached along highway MC 107 from the maritime oasis of Gabès. Here live cavemen of the desert,

dwelling in a cratered lunar landscape. From Matmata a more dubious track - the MC 104 - runs east to Médenine or west to the Saharan oases of Kebili and Douz, located on the dried-up shoreline of the huge salt-lake Chott Jerid. Most drivers prefer to back-track from Matmata to Gabès, to pick up the smoother highways - GP 1 to Médenine, or GP 16 to Kebili and Tozeur and thence to Nefta or northwards to the tiny mountain oases of Chebika and Tamerza.

Before rushing off to these main destinations, let's set the scene by looking closer at what makes life tick in the desert South - oases, camels and palm trees.

Oases

In Tunisia there are three quite distinctive types of oasis: maritime, mountain and desert. Their water sources are quite different: river, mountain springs or cascades, and springs that well up around the edges of huge salt lakes. Holidaymakers can explore all three types in a two-day or three-day safari from the coastal resorts.

The best-known maritime oasis is Gabès, easiest to reach along Tunisia's main trunk road, the GP 1. The oasis is served by the river water of Oued Gabès, which is fed by numerous springs. The coastal resort of Zarzis, facing Djerba, is also classed

73

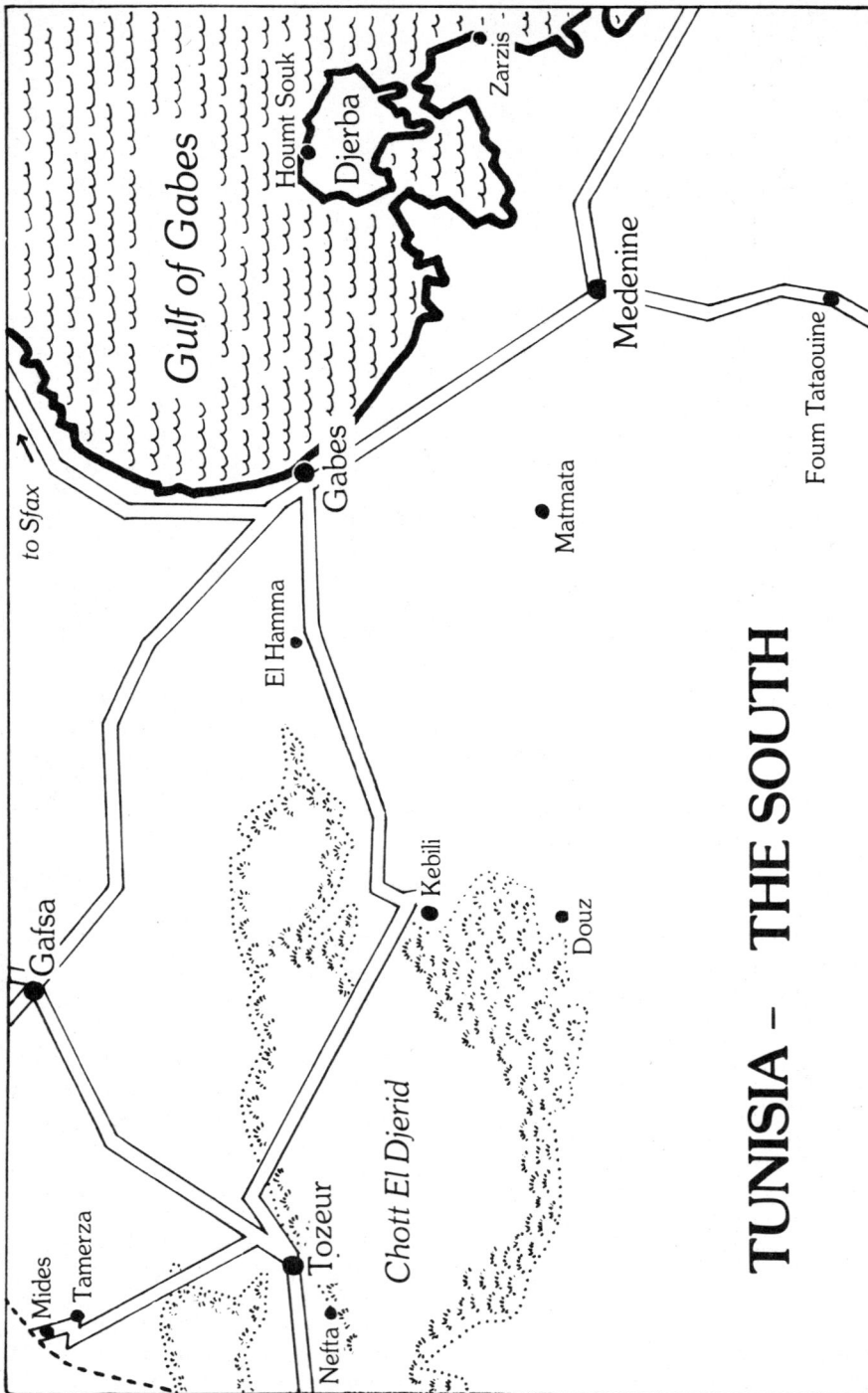

TUNISIA – THE SOUTH

Gulf of Gabes

to Sfax

Houmt Souk
Djerba
Zarzis

Medenine

Foum Tataouine

Gabes

Matmata

El Hamma

Gafsa

Kebili

Douz

Chott El Djerid

Mides
Tamerza

Tozeur

Nefta

as an oasis, but is really an enormous and very fertile olive grove.

Best examples of the archetypal oasis, hemmed in by sand, are Douz, Kebili, Tozeur and Nefta - all readily accessible along good roads that go around or across the dried-up salt lake of Chott Djerid. These oases are nourished by constant springs that give unbelievable life in contrast to the total desert of the wind-blown sand dunes.

Finally there are mountain oases, depending on springs and cascades that derive from the mountain range marking the border with Algeria. Gafsa is the largest and most important. The tiny oases of Chebika and Tamerza - only a few miles from the Algerian frontier - win out for sheer charm.

The oasis is an amazing gift of nature, especially when it blossoms in the midst of total desert. Typically, natural springs come bubbling up into a bowl of sand, with palm trees leaning over the shaded pool. The gurgling water is utterly dependable, and never runs dry.

From a hilltop you can survey the countryside. Wherever water flows there is rich, luxuriant greenery. Outside that perimeter is nothing but utterly barren rock and sand, where only snakes and scorpions can flourish.

The palm trees aren't there for mere cartoon decoration, but are an integral part of the working landscape, growing steadily thicker together as the desert boundary converts into a fully-fledged well-watered oasis.

For the most past, inhabitants build their dwellings just outside the greenery of the oasis, instead of within the beautiful shaded serenity of the oasis garden itself. The water-fed land of an oasis is too valuable to waste on house building.

Water is shared by a highly organised system laid down centuries ago. From its source, water ripples through canals which split up and sub-divide again, so that the whole oasis is laced with a network of streams. The owner of each plot of ground is entitled to water by the day, half-day or quarter-day, taken periodically. When his turn comes, the individual farmer opens up the canal leading to his land and blocks up his neighbour's canal, for which the turn has ended.

A typical one-hectare plot is luxuriant with trees, flowers and vegetables. Everything is cultivated by hand - no mechanization beyond camel-power! Between each planted bed, a channel is scooped out. Rivulets bubble along, switching first into one channel, then another. With water, an oasis-dweller can grow a rich variety of crops and trees: olives, apricots, pomegranates, bananas, plums, apples and grapes; rose-bushes, ablaze with colour; carrots, onions, peppers, garlic, beans, cucumbers, tomatoes and lettuce. There's even room for henna, so that women can paint their finger-nails, just like in Biblical times. When new irrigation is generated by sinking an artesian well, a bare patch of desert can be fully productive in five years.

The average oasis-dweller also owns livestock: maybe a dozen sheep, a camel, a donkey and a horse. Sometimes the animals are farmed out to pasture in the mountains, tended by Bedouin semi-nomads.

The oases, and the semi-arid areas, can sustain a remarkable amount of wildlife. Wherever there is water or vegetation, animals and birds come for their share. Flocks of birds roost in

75

belts of tamarisk which have been planted as defence against the incoming sands. Bee-eaters hover for insects. Fields of alfalfa are favourites of wagtails.

During migration seasons, storks welcome the chance to rest and preen. Other migrants include the egret and the glossy ibis. Desert sparrows build nests like weaver birds, and almost every oasis garden has a resident family of shrikes.

Palm Trees

Dominating the oasis scene is the date-palm, which has been something of a fertility symbol since ancient times. Palm trees serve many functions, of which the date harvest is not always the most important. Palms are also vital providers of shade. When the trees have grown towards maturity they can give shelter to smaller fruit trees - which, in turn, can then protect vegetable crops from the sun, while also acting as windbreak against desert sand-storms.

According to an Arab saying, date-palms grow 'with feet in the water and head in the sun.' In burning summer heat to ripen the fruit, every tree drinks 60,000 gallons of water a year. A good storm now and then is useless - indeed, a disadvantage, as rain lowers quality by over-swelling the pulp, and darkening the skin of the golden fruit.

Date palms are hand pollinated. The farmer plants only one lonely male tree to service all his female trees. In springtime he clambers up each palm with a male flower, and ties it close among the branches of female blossoms. This human-aided pollination is more effective than leaving it all to the vagaries of the wind, and ensures maximum setting of the date-flowers.

During summer the stems of dates hang down from the tops of the trees, and turn a golden brown colour around September. A typical oasis-dweller cultivates perhaps thirty date-palms. Normally several varieties are grown, ripening at different times to spread the harvest season.

At harvest time, there is complete division of labour. Men and boys clamber up the rough tree-trunks and hand down the heavy stems of dates from one to another. A good stem may carry a thousand fruits, weighing 20 pounds. Trees yield between 100 and 300 pounds of dates, according to season. The chain system continues even on ground level. Unripe dates are removed, and the harvest is transported by donkey-cart to a central store. The date-picking season - November and December - is the time for cheerful night-time festivities, with impromptu Arabic sing-songs, and snake-charmers tuning up their flutes.

The fruit is then graded at Cooperative packing stations. The best golden-skinned dates go into small boxes for export. Somewhat lower-quality dates are separated, to be exported in bulk for confectionery use.

In their original condition, dates vary widely in their moisture content. Some are so dry they can be carried loose in the pocket. Others are so swollen that they are almost melting. In the processing plants, the dates are transformed into a uniform product. On arrival, they are cleansed of dust and sand, and then sorted into hard, medium and soft. Dry dates are soaked to adjust their proportion of water to sugar. Over-swollen dates are dried in hot-air chambers. This conditioning ensures that export dates conform to a standard of roughly 66% weight of sugar - mainly glucose - and 24% water. Every box of dates is just as sticky as the next.

For local consumption, Tunisians eat mainly the dry varieties, which can be crisp enough to break. But these hard dates provide the same rich nourishment as in the familiar long, oval boxes.

The premium export variety is Deglet En Noor - 'Finger of Light' - renowned for its size, transparency and richness in sugar flavoured like honey. Growers distinguish over 100 varieties. Their names are a curious mixture of the poetic and the unexpected: 'Mother of the Master', 'Snake's-eye', 'Gazelle's Horns', 'Pigeon's-eye', 'Ox-brain', 'Housewife's Finger', 'Teeth of a Key', 'Donkey's Ear', 'Nostrils of Women'.

Commercial date-palms are not grown from date-stones, which would produce haphazard varieties and equal numbers of male and female trees. Too many males are a waste of productive land. Instead, growers use suckers that grow near the base of a parent tree and which replicate its sex and characteristics. When these offshoots are between 3 and 6 years old, and have established a root formation, they are replanted. Five years later they'll begin to yield, will reach maturity at age 20, and will continue bearing until they're a hundred years old, when yields dwindle.

While date-palms provide a major cash crop in the desert and mountain oases - particularly when the Deglet En Noor variety is intensively grown - they are still cultivated in maritime oases like Gabès, where quality is poor. Palms are planted to provide shelter for other crops. As a bonus, a mild and refreshing beverage called *laghmi* is made from date-palm sap. It starts non-alcoholic, but ferments within a day into a more potent palm toddy. The sap can also be boiled down for its sugar content.

Palm trees offers literally a cradle to the grave service. A newborn baby nestles in a cradle made from palm; later, palm trunks provide timber for house and furniture building; basketware is made from smaller leaves, and fuel and ropes are derived from the fruit stems; fibre makes cordage and packing material; palm fronds make fish traps off the islands of Kerkennah and Djerba. Finally an oasis-dweller can be buried in a palm-wood coffin.

Camels

To be strictly accurate, or pedantic, there are virtually no camels in Tunisia. A camel should have *two* humps, whereas the beasts you see throughout North Africa manage with only one. They are not camels, but dromedaries.

However, rightly or wrongly, everyone calls them camels, except for purists like Mr Majdi Salaheddine, assistant director of the Tourist Office in Tozeur. He comes from a long line of nomadic Berbers, and grew up among dromedaries. He boasts: 'I am the son of someone who had many, many dromedaries.' He is angry that guide-books never tell the full story of the camel - oops, dromedary!

Mr Salaheddine worked for years as a tour guide in the desert. He found that visitors always wanted to know (a) about the life-style of the camel and (b) about palm-trees. He was scornful of guide-books which gave people

77

none of that key background to what they see during a desert journey. The author of this chapter promised to redress the balance.

For instance, when crossing a desert area why do you often notice a group of camels, totally by themselves, with nobody watching over them? Are they wild? Or escaped?

Quite simply, a camel-owner just turns them loose to go grazing on their own. They move off into the surrounding desert for perhaps two or three days, before homing in back to base. Normally they always move towards the sun - going due east at first light, gradually veering south during the day, and finally westward towards sunset. They have a sensitive spot on the back of their neck which does not like over-exposure to the sun. This orientation pattern enables them to graze in comfort, while automatically steering them back in the general direction of where they started.

The herd always follows a leader dromedary - usually the oldest member of the troupe - who guides them where to eat and to drink. They cover 10 or 12 miles in a day's grazing. The leader dromedary will always return after several days to the tent of his nomadic owner, without any prompting or herding. However many in the herd - a dozen, or a score, or a hundred, male and female - there's never a single animal which goes missing.

Camels go best on sand. They have wide-spreading tender feet which do not like rocks or stones. Likewise, their legs are very brittle, and break easily if they stumble. So, generally, camels are not used in rocky terrain.

When camels mate, they will copulate only in privacy. If they are members of a herd, the male and female will prefer going behind a hill, out of sight of the others, and preferably by night. If a camel owner wants a selected pair to breed, he will often erect a tent where the bridal couple can mate in darkness and seclusion.

After giving birth, the female camel goes off by herself with her baby, at least a mile from the rest of the herd. It's a strange question of scent. If mother and child are forced to remain with other camels, then the newborn animal will surely die. About two months later, they both rejoin the herd. The young camel then starts learning the group skills of desert survival.

A female camel has a highly developed level of motherly love. If separated from the infant, her eyes will stream with tears and she moans her distress. When somebody dies - the head of a family, for instance - this trait is exploited by removing a mother camel from her newborn: whereupon she cries and cries inconsolably, with tears streaming down. In a pathetic way, she is used as a professional domestic mourner.

Camels are easily trained. As members of a herd, they soon understand from their elders what to do. They are ready for work at four years of age, reach maturity at sixteen and live for an average of forty. A camel can carry a 5-cwt load 25 miles a day, for three days without drinking. At a desert water-hole it can then fill up with twenty gallons.

Mr Majdi Salaheddine ends his panegyric: 'As a leader among domestic animals, the dromedary has no equal in being able to look after himself. All this is not legend or mythology, but reality. The full character of a dromedary is found in no other animal, from the rabbit until the lion.'

According to natural history experts, the one-humped Arabian camel (or dromedary) probably came originally from Central Asia. It arrived in the Nile Valley about 300 BC, but was not generally established further west until Christian times. This novel form of passenger and cargo transport did not become abundant in North Africa until at least 400 AD. With the growth of tourism, its survival in Tunisia's resorts and desert sites is assured.

Gabès

Mileage to Gabès: Tunis 230; Hammamet/Nabeul 215; Sousse 165; Monastir 150; 85; Djerba 80; Matmata 25; Tozeur 150; Gafsa 120; Medenine 50.

Gabès is far removed from the cartoon image of a pool, two palm-trees and a slumbering camel. Fed by the Oued Gabès, the oasis is densely packed with four square miles of greenery on the north side of the river. South side is the modern town, rebuilt after heavy damage during the North African campaign of 1943.

Entrance to the oasis is marked by souvenir stalls stacked high with handicrafts, including enough palm-leaf or straw hats to feed a thousand donkeys. You can wander on foot into the oasis and get lost amid the labyrinth of footpaths beneath the spiky shadows of palm trees. As a more popular and classic means of sightseeing, horse-drawn carriages await to transport visitors to the heart of the oasis at Chenini. No need to haggle: it's a fixed-price deal.

Taking a one-hour carriage ride is money well spent, giving you the extra height to see vignettes of oasis life over the hedges of palm fronds: boys playing football, women chattering as they pound clothes into submission at a communal washing-place, women farming in the crouch position as they tend their vegetable beds, men playing dominoes beside an idyllic shaded stream.

If you want to take pictures, best position is up beside the driver. Otherwise, choose an open-topped buggy. Sitting in a carriage with sun canopy can be irritating: a dangling fringe keeps dancing in front of your viewfinder. There's no risk of sunstroke! Within the oasis, an overall canopy of 300,000 palm trees provides thick shade.

In fact, shade-giving is the trees' main function. Gabès dates are of poor quality, owing to unwanted moisture in the air from proximity to the sea. The interlocking leaves of closely-planted palms have woven shelter from the burning heat for hundreds of tiny market gardens. Within each plot are lush plantings of all the Tunisian fruits, which co-exist with lower-level vegetables, tobacco and henna.

Gabès oasis is three or four miles across. The so-called 'Cascade' was first developed by the Romans who built a dam to create a shady pool, which now is converted into a concrete swimming pool. Close by there's a crocodile farm, and low-cost accommodation at the Chela Club. A halt on the carriage drive is marked by a cluster of stalls selling fruit, drink and general souvenirs. Tour-group convoys are greeted by local vendors, eagerly calling their wares - 'Apricots! Apricots!' or whatever is the seasonal fruit. Others are shouting 'Scorpions! Scorpions!' It sounds like some traditional chorus of welcome.

The oasis has a two-mile sea frontage,

but holiday development is modest compared with Tunisia's resorts to the north and on Djerba island. The Gulf of Gabès offers miles of powder-fine white sand, and the few hotels feature the usual water-sport facilities. Generally, though, the hotels are used for lunch stops and overnight transit for travellers on tours to the South. Using Gabès as the gateway, excursions are easy to the principal sightseeing destinations: Matmata, Médenine, Djerba, and the desert oases. For the go-it-alone traveller, Gabès is the southern terminus of the main railway line, but there are regular onward buses going south and west.

Principal hotels are the 556-bed two-star Chems, and the neighbouring three-star Oasis. The beach offers a direct view across to the heavy-chemical industrial zone. Other two-star hotels are the Nejib and the Tacapes. Recommended restaurants are: Le Pacha, La Ruche, l'Oasis, El Mazar, Le Casino, and El Khalij. Among local specialities are very large prawns.

Matmata

It's one of Tunisia's major tourist destinations: the underground village of Matmata, where the inhabitants prefer to be cavemen. The location is easily reached from the coastal oasis of Gabès, 29 miles into the Matmata Hills. After a series of hairpins along a blacktop road, you finally round a bend and look down on a broad moonscape valley, pitted with craters like the target area for carpet-bombing.

There's a cluster of official buildings, a mosque, the white-domed tomb of a Holy Man, scattered palm trees, and innumerable paths that wind across the valley between the craters. But

this is no abandoned troglodyte colony, carefully preserved as a curiosity by the Tourist Board. Whisps of smoke curl up from several of the gaping cavities. The above-ground shopping centre is thronged with tribesmen swathed in blankets or white sheets worn like Roman togas. They haggle over eggs, peppers or bolts of cloth. The parking lot is filled with donkeys and camels. Women walk along with robes flowing. Children pour out of school, clutching their satchels, running off down the paths and then disappearing into the giant shell-holes. Quite plainly, the cave-dwelling community of Matmata is still in active use.

Historically, there are three Matmata's. The original settlement, long since abandoned and in ruins, was perched upon two peaks which dominate the region. Easily defended, but hard of access, the caves were honeycombed into the mountain face.

Along the approach highway, you can still see examples of that building style, with various habitations carved into the soft terraced hillsides. Some consist of single vaulted rooms that tunnel into the rock face. You have a weird impression of passing through a village, without a single house in sight. Small patches of earth are cultivated, in between spasmodic palm and olive trees. Paths wind along terraces, and vanish into holes in the ground. But it's all just the aperitif for the fantastic sight as you suddenly get your view over the entire Matmata valley.

During the 17th century, with more settled local conditions, the Berber villagers moved down from their mountain-top dwellings into the broad valley that is present-day Matmata.

But then, around 1962, yet another New Matmata was developed - 800 three-roomed houses built by the Government, with the intention of evacuating holes-in-the-ground Matmata. The Government felt that cave-dwelling was not really a 20th-century image for Tunisia. But when the time came to move, local opposition mounted. The villagers would have been relocated 12 miles from their fields and trees, instead of a mere mile or two. Besides, most people thought their traditional burrows were far more practical for desert living. At the time, irritated officials talked of moving out the population by force, for their own good: new-style upward mobility, climbing out of the earth into above-ground houses. But finally the Government gave way, and any resettlement was voluntary. But gradually the younger generation is being tempted away by the affluent life-style of windows, flush toilets and a tiled kitchen.

There is great convenience about the Matmata cave-dwelling. Construction is simple, even though it demands far more hard work than building a conventional house. First you dig a pit, forty feet square and thirty deep. From twenty yards back, you construct a steeply-sloping entrance tunnel - high enough for camels - leading down to the pit floor, which forms the central courtyard. Burrowing into the sides of the crater, you hollow out rooms. Later, as the family grows, you dig a second level of bedrooms and storage chambers above the first, with steps hewn into the soft, easily-worked rock.

Well-established property owners become still more ambitious and build extensions. One room can lead into two or three others. Sometimes an entire new wing is added, with a communication tunnel to another courtyard. There are stables for the domestic animals. Goats are kept mainly to provide milk or white *feta*-type cheese, rather than meat.

Matmata even features an underground oil-press, where a two-centuries'-old machine is driven by a blindfolded camel who travels in a never-ending circle. In Sfax, oil extraction is done by machine, and 100% of the oil is extracted. By camel-power, the yield is only 80%. But nothing is lost, using old-fashioned methods. Pulp containing the remaining twenty percent of oil makes a nutritive cake, fed to the donkeys and camels throughout the year. Without this supplementary food for the animal work-force, how could the farmer harvest and transport his olives?

Caves keep warm in winter, cool in summer. They are well protected against dust and sand-storms, when the wind howls across the desert. The tradition is well established. Even the practical-minded Romans built underground villas in other parts of Tunisia, to escape the climatic extremes. Curiously, the only Matmatans who don't reside deep underground are the dead ones. They are buried in shallow ground-level tombs, thirty feet above a subterranean mosque.

There is nothing Stone Age about the 20th-century cave-dwellers. They dress in the same style as the average working citizen of oasis or town. Children stay at school till age 16 and take compulsory French as their main foreign language. But there is no local industry apart from traditional crafts, and many folk migrate to earn a seasonal living elsewhere.

The biggest problem is water. In the whole valley, natural wells or springs

81

are non-existent. Every family hoards drinking supplies in cisterns that collect the occasional rain. The only padlocks in Matmata are on the covers of private storage-tanks. When supplies run dry, water must be fetched from a source miles away.

Bright-eyed children invite you to view their underground homes in return for a small tip. Each barrel-vaulted cave is whitewashed. In store rooms, Ali Baba jars are filled with olive oil. Spotlessly clean bedrooms have ornaments ranged neatly along the walls. The main living-room is cool, well sheltered from the glare of the midday sun. Niches, shelves and working surfaces are 'built in' - hewn from the living rock.

Surrounded by chubby-faced children, womenfolk chatter as they roll balls of wool for their main 'cottage' industry of carpet-making. Hand-woven designs follow geometric Berber patterns that are quite unchanged from former centuries.

Tourism has helped preserve this relic of the past. Enough visitors arrive year-round to support a Hotel Marhala (which means 'rest-house') operated by the Touring Club of Tunisia, one or two other restaurants and cafés, the Hotel les Berbères, and another below-ground hostel named Sidi Driss. There's even a coiffeur. At souvenir stands, there are dried scorpions for sale - just the job for putting onto the pillow of your loved one. Large motor coaches park outside the Hotel Marhala, which is a good lunchtime pull-up for travelling cave-viewers.

If you dream of being an overnight caveman, b. & b. £2, Hotel Marhala is the pits, formed by several traditional crater dwellings linked together. Each first-floor barrel-vaulted bedroom cell is reached by shinning up with a rope.

For less agile guests, steps are hacked into the rock. You sleep in troglodyte rooms equipped with camp beds, and a switch for the dangling electric light bulb. The heavy bedroom door is built of palm planks, held together by olivewood pegs.

A standard main meal is all-Tunisian: bread and harissa to warm up your taste-buds while waiting for the peppery soup course, then a cheese and egg brik, and couscous reddened with more harissa sauce. All food and refreshment prices are very modest, in line with the facilities. For many visitors, the biggest attraction is that Matmata's moon landscape became an ideal film location for 'Star Wars', with interior scenes shot at the Marhala. Even with three hostelries, and a fourth due to open, Matmata is short on night-life. Mint tea and dominoes is about the wildest it gets.

Because of easy access along a good road, Matmata attracts the bulk of tourist visitors. But there are several similar settlements in the area. The most spectacular is Toujane, 15 miles to the east, along the MC 104 track towards Médenine. To explore the immediate area in greater depth, stay overnight in Matmata, and travel onwards by donkey, mule or jeep.

For exploration deeper south, or into the pure desert, careful planning is required. Outside of Matmata, Médenine and Tataouine, simple hostel accommodation and meals are available at Ksar Haddada near Ghomrassen, and at Chenini - all accessible by a regular self-drive car. But if you intend to venture off the hard-topped roads and dirt tracks, it's sensible to use a Land Rover with a guide or driver who is experienced in Saharan travel. Anyway, venturing into the Sahara zones is permissible only if you first contact the National Guard Post in Médenine, stating your planned route, and where you expect to depart from the region.

During the 11th century, the original Berber tribesmen retreated from the invading Arab hordes of the Beni Hillal. Taking refuge on mountain tops, they burrowed cave dwellings into near-perpendicular cliffs that became like human ant-hills. Thence they could venture down onto the plains and valleys, tending their herds of sheep and goats, growing wheat or barley, and harvesting olives and figs.

Vaulted storage chambers were built, and the larger groups of *ghorfas*, piled one upon the other, became granary castles called *ksars*, up to six storeys high around a central courtyard. Later, when more settled conditions returned, the Berber villagers rebuilt lower down the mountainside and even onto the plain. If you have the time, a visit to the Deep South reveals an entirely different world from the Mediterranean coastline.

Kebili

En route from Gabès along highway GP 16, there are several small oases such as El Hamma, where the Romans came for the hot spa waters, 117°F and slightly sulphurous. Finally, fringing the shore of Chott Djerid, numerous little oases focus on the administrative centre of Kebili.

Of course, the Romans came here, for Kebili has strategic value, commanding the traditional trading routes. Kebili has a higher-than-average population of negro origin, dating from past centuries of trans-Saharan slave trade. Thousands were imported to work the land, where formerly the mosquito count was high, with malaria endemic.

For the 20th-century traveller, Kebili is a pleasant refreshment stop, possibly at the Hotel Fort des Autruches, converted and upgraded from its ex Foreign Legion days. 'Autruches' is French for 'Ostriches', who would probably enjoy all those lovely sand-drifts. In the oasis centre are natural swimming pools where children bathe joyously while mothers pound the family wash. Virtually every house in the oasis has a television aerial sprouting from the roof. Kebili is firmly into Deglet en Noor cash-crop territory, with palms planted close together to maximise the yield per garden.

From Kebili, towards Tozeur, mini-oases line the road that passes by the edge of Chott el Djerid. They offer delightful green havens from the sand-drifts. Notice the patterned brick construction - the traditional building style of the Djerid. Keep alert for all the little glimpses of oasis life: a sheep grazing, tethered to a peg; a man kneeling in prayer towards Mecca, with his prayer mat unrolled in a tiny patch of shade; semi-nomadic Bedouins, leading a string of camels.

Douz

Fifteen miles due south of Kebili is Douz, labelled as the Gateway to the Desert. If it's Thursday, go there for the weekly market, where semi-nomads offer camels for sale, or socks made of wool and goat hair for walking on the desert sands. During winter - check the precise date - Douz vibrates with the annual Festival of the Sahara, held near the golden sand dunes of El Hofra. There are poetry contests, camel fights and *fantasias* - thrilling charges on horseback accompanied by war-cries and gunfire. Modest no-star accommodation is available, mostly chalet-style or under canvas. A camel ride on the dunes is obligatory, for the sake of all your friends who are looking forward to seeing your holiday snaps.

Chott el Djerid

Crossing this huge salt-lake is an experience in itself. Formerly it was a hazardous journey, following a marked track that was open to wheeled traffic only during the dried-up months from March onwards. Anyone who wandered off-trail would flounder in a black quagmire beneath a topping of salt. But today there's a proper asphalted road, built on a causeway just above the salt-pan.

Everyone wants to see a mirage, and the journey across the Chott el Djerid virtually guarantees a sighting. Mirages are at their most plentiful around midday or one o'clock, when the sun is highest. Across the flat surface, encrusted with minerals that sparkle in the sun, you pick out a line of palm trees, growing above water which isn't there. Phantom lakes look remarkably real, shimmering in the haze. But you soon learn it's no use asking the driver to turn off for a swim.

Notice that the water which gathers in the trench on each side of the causeway is of a different colour. On the right, driving towards Tozeur, the water is brownish; on the left, it's green or blue. The causeway operates like a dam. The right-hand ditch fills with water from the tawny mountains to the north; on the left it's pure salt water from the Chott itself, thick with white crystals.

Along the highway are occasional rock-hound stalls selling 'desert rose' rocks, mineral waters for those who fear death from thirst, and WC blocks for travellers who, despite everything, are near to bursting. You have to be desperate.

Then, quite suddenly, the totally bare soil of the Chott gives place to vegetation - at first scattered, but rapidly becoming green enough to support scattered herds of sheep and goats. Next there are palm trees ahead. It's not a mirage, but a charming string of small oases called El Ouadiane, meaning 'The Waddies'. The six villages are virtually an outpost of Tozeur, largest of the Tunisian oases.

If you're approaching Tozeur from the north - along highway GP 3 from Gafsa - the outpost oasis is El Hamma du Djerid. Hot springs, slightly above blood temperature, made this a favourite spa resort of the Romans. Even today, people take the cure.

Tozeur

Mileage to Tozeur: Tunis 280; Hammamet 244; Sousse 185; Gafsa 60; Nefta 15; Gabès 150; Djerba 230; Kebili 55.

Capital of the Djerid region, Tozeur claims around 200,000 palm trees, watered by 132 streams fed by some 200 springs. The irrigation system for the four square miles of oasis was established in 13th century by a wise man called Ibn Chabbat. The water-sharing system was rigorously fair and still works perfectly, with friendly cooperation between neighbours.

A delight is to go strolling through the oasis. The atmosphere is tranquil. There's the clip-clop of donkey hooves that kick up little spurts of dust, while their rider listens to the morning news in Arabic on his Sony Walkman. Donkey carts are fitted with thick rubber tyres. A greybeard cycles along

84

at a stately 6 m.p.h. Through a maze of date-palm plantations and vegetable gardens, you can reach one of the many sources of water, springing forth at 85°F. For the best overall view of Tozeur, aim for the rocky hill called the Belvedere.

Most of Tozeur's buildings keep to a unique local style of construction with desert-yellow bricks. Making maximum use of light-and-shade patterns produced by the brilliant sunlight, bricks are laid with ends protruding in a style that originated many centuries ago. The simple but varied geometric designs are very similar to those woven into most local fabrics, blankets and carpets.

Some buildings date from the 14th century, when Tozeur was a major trading centre with up to 100,000 inhabitants. Tozeur's history goes much further back, particularly to Roman times when the outpost of Tusuros was on the Roman line of march from Gabès to Biskra. Later, the Berber population became devout Christians, and held out against the Islamic tide for a hundred years. Today, Tozeur numbers only 15,000 people, though the population is possibly growing again with the combined effects of tourism, better communications and the increase in oasis area through sinking of artesian wells. Main Street, Tozeur, was widened and rebuilt 20-odd years ago, mostly with facades that follow the traditional style. There's a well-equipped date-farmers' Cooperative and packing plant, a covered market, several banks, a Town Hall and a desert bus terminal. The Great Mosque dates from 11th century, with its minaret built on Roman foundations.

As a thriving centre of tourism,

Tozeur features a good range of hotels, including a 3-star Grand Hotel of the Oasis, the Club Med's Hotel Ras El Ain, and a PLM hotel next door.

There are two zoos in Tozeur - Tijeni's Zoo and the Paradise Garden. To call them zoos is rather pushing it. Certainly they can show you some live and pickled scorpions, horned vipers and chameleons. Specially interesting is a desert lizard called *waran*, who dines off scorpions. Local people ensure that a *waran* is literally attached to their house and garden, by tying him with a long thread round a leg. Apart from these attractions, Paradise is worth visiting for its well-tended collection of fruit-trees, shrubs, date-palms and flowers. Fascinating for any gardener!

The rival desert zoo was founded by Tijeni Jegelle who built a prosperous business, catching snakes and scorpions and exporting them to research institutes around the world. Especially he sold to laboratories, where venom was extracted to make snake-bite serum. The zoo is now operated by Tijeni's son.

Nefta

From Tozeur it's only a brief 14-mile drive across a desert highway to Nefta, with views away left over the glistening saltpans of Chott el Djerid, with good chance of mirage-spotting. Along the approaches into Nefta, the first hotel on the left is Hotel Le Nomade, which reads as Hotel Lemonade at a quick, thirsty glance. Further along - near a classic viewpoint on the rim of the Corbeille - is Hotel Mirage, but it's really there, quite solid.

Nefta's top-ranking hotel is close by,

the 4-star Sahara Palace - part of the French PLM group - devoted to luxury-grade desert tourism. The pool terrace offers a superb view over La Corbeille - a deep 2,500-acre Basket or Bowl filled with 350,000 palm-trees fed by 150 natural springs, boosted by artesian wells. In the foreground are tents where tourists can be entertained like desert nomads. Nefta is famed for its folk-dances. The Sabre, Rifle and Stambali Dances are performed to the shattering rhythm of big drums, tambourines and castanets.

Across the green sea of La Corbeille, on the background hillside, are the white buildings of Nefta. With about 15,000 inhabitants, Nefta is the region's most thickly populated oasis. Mosques and white-domed *marabouts* - tombs of saints - are numerous, for Nefta is also a major religious centre for the Sufi sect which practises deep meditation, mysticism and the worship of holy men.

The hotel precincts are launching-pad for camel or donkey safaris through the oasis, or by camel or jeep to the sand-dunes. The highway to the Beau Geste fantasy of scalloped dunes gives another overview of the oasis, meeting the desert in a sharp dividing line. Even on the main tarred highway, each vehicle produces its little wind-sock of dusty sand.

Off-trail, onto the sand-dunes, is a thrill, demanding a similar expertise to driving on snow. Unless you're in a vehicle with four-wheel drive, it's easy to get stuck. When the vehicle stops for picture-making, a lurking camel driver will materialize out of the sands, to charge one dinar per person for sitting aboard his camel.

At another desert pull-up for Land Rovers, cool shelters from the sun are made with palm trunk supports, and thatched with palm fronds. Refreshment stands offer tea made with pure mineral water. A dozen stalls display big chunks of 'sand roses' or 'desert roses' - naturally formed out of brown barite.

Tamerza

Forty miles from Tozeur along highway GP 16, Tamerza is approached by a series of hairpin bends that twist like Arabic calligraphy into a wildly beautiful mountain landscape of razor-backed ridges and dramatic canyons. Part of the highway has reverted to its original gravel base, and the scenery is pure spaghetti Western. On the fringe of the oasis is a ghost village. This was the original Tamerza, abandoned in 1969 when - quite incredibly - it was inundated by torrential floods.

There is sheer delight in the huge contrast between rugged desert and the lovely greenery of this mountain oasis. Dense cultivation is fed by a warm-water cascade. Hotel Cascade offers bamboo-hut bedrooms with swimming pool and an outdoor restaurant. After lunch, if your Land Rover has been sitting in the sun, you'll learn what it's like to be a microwave chicken.

A few miles away is Chebika, which depends on a similar cascade. The resulting stream flows through a mini canyon like a magic elixir, carpeting the canyon floor with a green paradise of palm trees and vegetable gardens. In several idyllic locations, visitors can cool off in the waters.

Metlaoui

Roughly halfway between Gafsa and Tozeur are the scarred hillsides of Metlaoui, tinted with vivid colours and rich in phosphates. These deposits were first reported in 1885 by a French vetinerary scientist called Philippe Thomas, who specialized in doctoring goats. Ten years later, when demand for phosphate-based fertilizers boomed, Tunisia rapidly became one of the world's largest producers. Exports are trundled out by rail through Sfax.

A tourist train called The Red Lizard starts every day from the town of Metlaoui. The journey up the Gorges of Selja lasts one hour 30 minutes in 1904-vintage carriages which originally belonged to the Bey of Tunis. One can sample oriental splendour, with accompanying music, as the train chugs up the gorge (mainly tenanted by snakes and scorpions, in case you think of hiking up to save the fare).

Gafsa

Mileage to Gafsa, from Tunis 220; Bizerta 260; Hammamet 190; Sousse 165; Kairouan 125; Djerba 230; Tozeur 60.

Originally a Berber stronghold, in Roman times this mountain oasis was named Capsa. Little now remains of the ancient Roman town, apart from swimming pools that are still in use by local schoolkids, who dive for tourist coins. Odd fragments of Roman buildings are embedded in the Kasbah walls and in some private dwellings.

The town's importance continues, standing at the dividing-line between Tunisia's grain-growing and date-growing zones. For strategic reasons, Gafsa is still a garrison town, just like in the Roman era, besides ranking as the administrative capital of southwest Tunisia. During the last war, Gafsa changed hands several times in 1943,

and the 15th-century kasbah was severely damaged by a munitions explosion. Local talent for geometric design shows in the decorative bricklaying on public and private buildings.

Today, the peaceful oasis claims 300,000 low-yield date palms which primarily give shade to a range of quality fruit including citrus, apricots, figs and grapes.

What to buy

On the shopping front, Gafsa is famed for its traditional hand-woven woollen blankets and Mergoum carpets, coloured with dazzling geometric patterns and childlike designs of stylised animals and people. The red and white striped blankets are called *battaniyas*; the patterned blankets with figures are *farrachiyas*.

Available in the Gabès area are handwoven and embroidered wool hangings, rugs, shawls and saddle cloths. Colours are home-dyed in the wool, using vegetable dyes made from safran, henna, indigo leaves, pomegranate skin, nut shells or oak bark. All these items can be bought any day, but the market area is liveliest on Sundays.

In Tozeur and Nefta, merchants offer various handwoven fabrics in wool, silk or cotton, such as *Haiks*, *Foutas* and *Malahfas*. These comprise the traditional costume of Bedouin women, and are great for your next fancy dress party. Otherwise they can be used as tablecloths, curtains or bedspreads.

Other Bedouin and Berber products are silk scarves and embroidered girdles, and pile carpets.

8. The Inland Sites

Whether your holiday base is in the Hammamet area, or Sousse and Monastir, it's well worth taking a sightseeing swing into the interior of Tunisia. Easiest of access are Kairouan and El Djem, particularly from the resorts around Sousse. But a worthwhile day can be spent on a circuit of other major sites which primarily are relics of the great centuries of Roman colonization, when Tunisia was the richly productive breadbasket of Rome.

Popular whole-day itineraries aim for Dougga, with halts en route at Zaghouan and Thurburbo Majus. Sbeitla is sometimes included on longer safaris to the South. A dedicated enthusiast could easily spend a week's self-drive, covering much higher mileage to visit Bulla Regia, Maktar and more of the Punic sites.

Whichever you choose, you'll see a good cross-section of the Tunisian countryside: wide areas of grain crops, now farmed with modern machinery; extensive fruit orchards and olive groves, fenced with prickly pear; and dusty villages, where donkey transport still rules.

Kairouan

If you can spare only a single half-day from beach sun-worship, Kairouan is the sightseeing tour to pick. Among Tunisia's inland sites, Kairouan easily gets top rating for a life-style and a town landscape that is totally different from anything in Europe. As the fourth holiest city in the Islamic world - after Mecca, Jerusalem and Medina - Kairouan is the most important place of pilgrimage in North Africa. Among the faithful, seven visits to Kairouan equal once to Mecca.

This holy status dates back to 671 AD, when the Arab conqueror Okba Ibn Nafaa - a companion of the Prophet Mohammed - halted his troops amid a barren plain and proclaimed: 'this is an ideal spot on which to build a stronghold for Islam, capable of surviving until Judgement Day.' He also made a speech to the wildlife, and his words are credited with driving out scorpions and vipers from the area, leaving it free for building of a garrison town which became the capital of western Islam.

There were good strategic reasons for the location: on an open plain, distant from the Berber tribes in the mountains and from the Byzantine fleets that harassed the coastline. During the early centuries of Arab rule, splendid monuments were built, particularly during a 9th-century Golden Age. Over the centuries, Kairouan has kept its Arab character intact: mosques, bazaars, ramparts, cobbled lanes; Islamic traditions and crafts. Infidels were not encouraged to settle.

With so much to see, and the

highlights scattered in different corners of the sprawling city, it's best to take an organised coach tour. Otherwise, on foot, you'll need most of a day to explore the city walls, two or three mosques, the souks and the carpet industry. Whether you choose to take the standard tour, or to go-it-alone, the effort is rewarding, giving you an idea of the magnificence of Kairouan from its foundation over 1300 years ago.

If you are organising your own sightseeing, arriving by road from Sousse, Hammamet or Tunis, stop first at the Aghlabite Basins, just outside the perimeter of Kairouan. These are two large reservoirs, constructed 11 centuries ago during the great days of the Aghlabite dynasty to give the town a constant water supply. The larger pool holds 13 million gallons. Restored thirty years ago, their water is rich with algae, just perfect for local youths to use as a free swimming pool. Close by is a housing estate for resettled Bedouins.

After that, you can go directly opposite into the centre of town, past a decrepit kasbah on the left, through to the Tunis Gate - Bab et Tounes. Straight ahead leads into the shopping area: a fairly wide main thoroughfare with stores catering both for local people and visitors.

Make sure you find the Bir Barouta, in the very centre of the old town. Signs point the way, but can easily be missed. Ask a static shopkeeper to put you on course. Up some steps, and there's a blindfolded camel trudging round and round to draw water from a well. It's worth studying the engineering, based on 17th-century technology. According to legend, this well water comes direct from Mecca, but it's no longer used

for drinking. However, you're just as likely to see desert Bedouins, who come to taste this holy water. There's no entrance fee, but the keeper expects a small tip.

In order to visit the three main mosques, you must first get a strip of three admission tickets, price about 50p. These are obtainable from the Tourist Office on the southern end of town, at Place de l'Indépendance, where you can also hire an authorised local guide. All this is arranged by the Association for the Preservation of the Medina of Kairouan.

To get tickets, visitors must sign an undertaking 'to observe inside the mosque precincts decent dress, correct behaviour, and especially not to make any noise nor to create any disorder, and not to smoke, and not to walk on the mats, and not to enter into the prayer hall.' On coach tours, the guide signs on behalf of his entire party, and has to ensure that these rules are followed.

From this location, you can follow round the city walls for a ten-minute walk to the Great Mosque - either outside, on a broad, encircling boulevard, well swept; or inside the walls, where the unmade roads are well endowed with litter. The inside route is more interesting, offering little vignettes of local life, with occasional views through open doorways into the courtyards of private houses. Continue to the third gate, and then you see the Great Mosque of Sidi Okba - the fifth to stand on the present site.

The building has all the simplicity and grandeur that makes dramatic architecture. The inspiration for it, as well as the materials, were all borrowed. But the ensemble is breath-taking. The massive pylon minaret, from whence the faithful are called to prayer, derives from Egypt; the inside of the domes from Christianity. The four hundred pillars of the prayer hall are looted Roman and Byzantine, Ionic and Corinthian side by side - the long ones sawn to size, and the short mounted on pedestals. Inscriptions to the pagan gods of Rome and Greece fill odd spaces in the wall. Like the town of Kairouan itself, the Great Mosque is a hotchpotch of classic fragments that yet, surprisingly, achieves harmony. The whole mosque is alive with the sound of birds. They flutter and twitter within the prayer hall, enjoying the shade and perching on chandeliers.

Formerly, a Museum of Islamic Art was located opposite the Great Mosque entrance; but this has now been moved to Rakada, about 5 miles out on the GP 2 highway towards Sfax.

In the western corner of town is the Sidi Sahbi Mausoleum. Sidi Sahbi was a holy man who had acquired three hairs from the prophet Mohammed's beard. Hence he was given the name of The Barber, and his burial place is popularly known as the Barber's Mosque. You go through several courtyards before reaching the main courtyard which gives a very limited view into the prayer hall. The main attraction is the rich decoration of stylized tiles which go round every wall of the courtyards, which also are decorated with beautifully crafted friezes and stucco work.

A short distance away is the Sidi Amor Abbada mausoleum, built in 19th century by a nutty blacksmith who specialised in big and useless metal objects, including an anchor designed to stop Kairouan drifting away from Tunisia.

The principal industry of Kairouan is carpet-making, of which you'll get plentiful reminders. For an idea of prices, visit the ONAT building which is close to the Information Office, in a parallel side street. There you'll find a tremendous display of carpets and handicrafts at fixed prices. If you're in the market for carpet-buying, read the shopping notes in Chapter 12 of this book. Take traveller cheques, credit cards or hard currency for a discount on major purchases.

El Djem

The Colosseum at El Djem is easily the most impressive Roman monument in North Africa. Its design is almost identical to that of Rome's Colosseum. Certainly El Djem's version is in much better condition, being spared the traffic pollution which is Rome's big problem. Stonework is pristine in the crystal-clear sparkling air.

The setting is dramatic, at a crossroads midway across an empty plain. You can't miss it! The enormous building can be seen miles away, whether you arrive along the GP 1 highway which follows the basic Roman road between Sousse and Sfax; or along the equally straight roads from Mahdia on the coast, or Kairouan inland.

Today El Djem is just a modest market town with a railway station, but in Roman times the city of Thysdrus was a major centre for the lucrative olive oil trade. Even today, the main highway to Sfax passes through a 'Sea of Olives'. Wealthy merchants built luxury villas, virtually carpeted with mosaics. During the peak of city prosperity, early in 3rd century AD, the 35,000-capacity Colosseum - rated as 6th largest in the world - was built to replace a smaller amphitheatre located about 800 yards to the south. Decline dates from 238 AD, when a revolt against taxes ended in a frenzy of destruction by Roman soldiers sent in to restore order. The city never really recovered. Its power and prosperity was lost to Sufetela - present-day Sbeitla. When the Vandals arrived in 430, they had only a small settlement to pillage.

Until 1695, the Colosseum survived intact. It was then severely wrecked by order of the government, irritated by its occasional use as a fortress where tax-dodgers could hold out against tax collectors. In addition, the monument endured the usual fate of being treated as a handy stone-quarry.

This was justified by a legend that stones from the arena were proof against scorpions: so every local house needed this protection. Today, restoration is in full swing, jointly financed by the Gulbenkian Foundation and the Tunisian government.

Gladiator and wild animal fights were the main attraction. In the basement is the system of cages and tunnels essential to putting on a good show. At the Museum, located half a mile southwest, mosaics depict highlights of the performance: a lioness devouring a boar; a tiger charging a bull; a lion bringing down an antelope; panthers dining off a Christian; blood everywhere.

The Museum is laid out in Roman villa format and is mainly devoted to mosaic finds from the area. Picture subjects are principally game, hunting, wild animals, fish and fruit. A typical mosaic, wall-hung like a tapestry, depicts the Four Seasons - so splendidly portrayed that one half expects Vivaldi's music to break out

any moment. There's the usual pottery collection of Roman and Christian oil lamps dating mainly from the 4th century.

Adjoining the museum building is an excavated area of luxury Roman villas. This was an up-market residential area, even though the villas were back-to-backs. They all had running water, bathrooms, dining rooms, bedrooms - everything to make an estate agency drool over these very desirable homes with fitted mosaics. The mosaic floors glow in the sunshine, and well-matured villa gardens are planted in the original Roman style.

More unusual is a pigeon coot which could house about 30 pigeons if they were living single; or presumably 60 or more if cohabiting. They were used for the Roman pigeon-post system.

There's also a fine stretch of original Roman road, some 18 feet wide, paved, and it went straight through to Egypt. Shops lined both sides of the highway, just like the souvenir stores and cafés in El Djem today. Close to the Museum is an Arab well dating from 8th century. Alongside is a huge drinking trough - a camel-bar which could easily serve twenty camels, standing shoulder to shoulder. It was a good pull-in for caravans.

Zaghouan

From the coastal resorts, a popular one-day circuit of Roman Tunisia aims for Dougga as the main highlight, with visits en route to Zaghouan and Thurburbo Majus to stimulate the appetite.

Whether you start from the Hammamet or the Sousse area, the journey begins by travelling along highway GP 1, which follows the same alignment as the Roman road of 2nd century AD. That basic Roman road still continues right through to Alexandria in Egypt. Much of the route in Tunisia is flanked with eucalyptus trees, introduced into Tunisia from Australia during French rule, to provide shade.

From Hammamet, the MC 35 route towards Zaghouan turns off at Bou Ficha. During French occupation, this was a major military centre. From the Sousse direction, the MC 133 turns off near Enfidaville, the scene of fighting during the North African campaign. Most of the farmland is in private ownership, though some territory is State property. Formerly these lands were occupied by French colonists, but were distributed to local peasants soon after independence.

The approach to Zaghouan is heralded by the sight of dramatic mountains that look like mini-Dolomites, with jagged, fever-chart peaks that rise to 4,000 feet. The wide-spreading plain was part of the rich granary of Rome, watered by the Jebel Zaghouan in the background. Today, the character of the area has not changed. Grain, olive trees and fruit are still the main source of farm income.

It's well enough known that the Romans were great engineers. Their assignment at Zaghouan was typical of the huge projects they tackled. The lower slopes of the mountain gush with springs of sparkling cold water. About forty miles away by the seashore, the city of Carthage was inhabited by 700,000 people who couldn't possibly meet their domestic needs just from rainfall. Hence the enormous project of building a 40-mile aqueduct - representing a vast capital investment even by today's civil engineering standards. The volume

delivered was also sufficient to supply the beachside Baths of Antoninus at Carthage.

The present-day spa town of Zaghouan is pleasant and prosperous - a green oasis, in contrast to the semi-arid appearance of the surrounding countryside. The original Roman town was destroyed by the Vandals at the end of the 3rd century.

Tour coaches stop at the Nymphean, the Temple of Waters, built in 2nd century AD above the prodigious spring which was main supplier of water to Carthage. With time for refreshment at a café alongside, visitors can enjoy the superb setting of this theatrical monument against its backdrop of towering mountains. On the two wings of the Temple, colonnades held niches for a dozen statues that represented months of the year. The huge semi-circular marble fountain ends with a gigantic basin - a reservoir formed by two overlapping circles, where the water was collected for onward transmission by aqueduct.

A short distance out of Zaghouan, a few ground-level sections of the Roman aqueduct are visible. Elsewhere, nearer Tunis, the great Roman arches of the ruined aqueduct stride majestically across valleys. Today, Zaghouan still supplies Tunis, along a pipeline which follows the same basic alignment chosen by the Romans.

Thurburbo Majus

The highlight of Thurburbo Majus is the Capitol, built in 168 AD and dedicated to the three Roman deities - Jupiter, Juno and Minerva. Rated among the most beautiful in Africa, the Capitol towers on a massive platform above the Forum and other temples and public buildings. Just like elsewhere in Tunisia, the Vandals enjoyed smashing statues. Neglect, time and stone-robbing have finished off their work. Jupiter's statue stood 25 feet high, but only his head and his foot have survived. These mortal remains are now in the Bardo Museum.

Seat yourself on the steps of the Capitol, and survey the scene. In front is the square Forum, which was surrounded by Corinthian columns and a great wall. Around this Forum are the principal monuments. To the immediate right is the Temple of Mercury, the god of merchants and the corn trade on which the city's prosperity so much depended. In the right-hand corner is the market-place, with a paved courtyard laid out for 21 arcaded shops around three sides. At the opposite corner is the Curia, a two-roomed meeting place for the municipal senate and council.

Further over, beyond the market-place, are two Roman Baths - the Summer Bath and the Winter Bath.

Stroll across towards the Summer Bath, and you come first to the Palestra - a gymnasium and sport centre built for the younger generation. This public facility was donated in 225 AD by the rich Petronii family, who gave their name to the Portico of the Petronii. Black marble columns are well preserved, but decoration and statues have been removed to the Bardo. A delightful mosaic of two boxers, who look plump and in need of the exercise, is one of the Museum's great treasures. In the far right corner is a paving stone carved for a popular Roman pastime called the Thirtysix Letters Game. Letters are set around the board in

groups of six, so that it could almost double as a backgammon board. A few bits of mosaic remain in the summer baths alongside.

Close by is the Sanctuary of Baal, which serves as reminder that originally this was a Punic town, based on a Berber settlement. Initially a site was dedicated to the Punic goddess, Tanit - the grim deity who required a periodic sacrifice of first-born children. The Roman version of the cult used animals instead. In later Roman centuries, several temples on the site switched allegiance, and became churches.

Dougga

The route towards Dougga continues cross-country along MC 47, through Bou Arada and following the basic route of a railway line. One section of the road is dead straight; and, of course, that is precisely the line of the original Roman road to Dougga.

The Dougga site is reached via Teboursouk, where the fertile land is blessed with good rains, and a plentiful supply of river water. The flat terrain is idea for use of agricultural machinery, though some smaller farmers remain faithful to donkey power. Here is part of the 'granary of Rome', which gave settlers the wealth for their lavish villas and public buildings. From several miles away, the columns of Dougga rear up on a hillside, silhouetted against the skyline.

The hilltop site was already important in the Punic age, and later became a Roman colony. Most of Dougga's Roman monuments were erected in the 2nd or 3rd centuries AD, when the city of some 10,000 people was developing rapidly. Then troubles and decline came in early 4th century, and the inhabitants drifted off in favour of Teboursouk, four miles away. The first serious excavations were undertaken by French archaeologists from 1899 onwards, and today the site comes under the wing of the National Institute of Art and Archaeology in Tunis. Dougga is the pearl of Tunisia's Roman sites, the largest and best preserved.

Spread over its 60-acre site, Dougga rises in tiers up the south-facing crest of a hill at around 2000-ft altitude.

Up from the parking lot, the first major building is the Theatre, built in 168 AD and funded by a wealthy local family called Macii. Restored in 1910, the 3,500-seat Theatre is the elegant setting every year for the summertime Dougga Festival of classical plays - an event of international calibre. The acoustics are excellent, aided by earthenware pots which were embedded in the upper walls. As you look down from the topmost tiers, a splendid panorama opens up through the Corinthian colonnade - olive trees in the foreground, down to wheat-fields in the plain below. That landscape has not changed from 2,000 years ago.

From the Theatre, an ancient street leads along to The Square of the Winds - so named because of a compass-type inscription with the twelve names of the winds, as known to the Romans. To the right are the remains of the Temple of Mercury, the god of commerce. Left is the market-place, which Mercury protected.

The superb building ahead is the Capitol, dedicated to the classic Roman triad - the gods Jupiter, Juno and Minerva, with niches that indicate where their statues stood. The monument dates from 166 AD, funded by the same family of benefactors who paid for the Theatre. Very well preserved, the six honey-coloured Corinthian columns make a good photo subject. Above, in the temple pediment, a relief sculpture depicts a man being carried off to some Roman heaven by an eagle - the bird which always symbolised the Roman state. The subject of this uncomfortable form of transport was Emperor Antoninus Pius, who had died a few years' earlier, in 161 AD. Stacked against the inside wall of the Capitol is a good selection of inscribed tablets which finally give classicists a chance to prove the value of having learned Latin.

The standard Roman pattern was always to locate the Forum in front of the Capitol. Dougga is the exception. Owing to the nature of the terrain, the Forum is positioned at the side. With their preference for an orderly city-centre layout and grid-pattern streets, the Romans normally preferred to build on level ground - not on hill slopes like at Dougga. But then Dougga was already a well-established town before the Roman colonists arrived.

A reminder of that earlier civilization is the Temple of Juno Caelestis - Heavenly Juno. In pre-Roman times, she was worshipped under the Punic name of Tanit. As the Mother of Harvests, Celestial Juno is appropriately sited among olive trees.

Next to the 3rd-century Licinian Baths, built according to the universal Roman pattern, is the House of Dionysos and Ulysses. That name comes from the theme of two famous mosaics that are now re-housed in the Bardo Museum. The picture is often reproduced of Ulysses, tied to his ship's mast as he listens spellbound to the song of the Sirens, while his crew wear ear-plugs.

Next is the House of Trifolium, which looks like the remains of a medieval cloister - rectangular, with columns to support a covered ambulatory, and small rooms leading off each side. One can imagine serious-minded Romans pacing around the cloister, stopping for a little chat here and a little chat there. Obviously it must have been a beautiful place for monastic-style meditation - except that very explicit mosaics have identified the building as a brothel. Today the mosaics are housed in the Bardo, telling us all about the goings-on.

Close by is a well-designed street sign, indicating which way to the brothel: using a carved phallus as the pointer. Also in the neighbourhood are the Cyclops Baths, which included a 12-seater public toilet system. Constantly running water carried away the offerings.

From this general area there's a good view down to the Lybico-Punic Mausoleum, the pointed-tower monument at the foot of the hill, dating from 2nd-century BC. The 60-ft funerary tower on its square base survived the Romans, the Vandals and the Arabs, but collapsed in 1842 when a dedicatory plaque was torn down and shipped to the British Museum. The snatch was organised by the British Consul in Tunis. In those days, it was quite acceptable for Britain to do such things. Like the Rosetta Stone, the dedication to a Numidian king was carved in two languages - Phoenician and Numidian - a treasured find for scholars. The monument was restored by the French earlier this century, but the plaque remains in the British Museum as the 'inalienable property of the British people'.

Bulla Regia

Further across towards the Algerian border is Bulla Regia, almost as impressive as Dougga but much less visited for reasons of location. With a self-drive car or on a dedicated coach tour, the extra distance is worth while. But it's not really feasible on a one-day swing from the holiday coastline.

The curiosity is that much of Bulla Regia is built underground, for the same persuasive climatic reasons as for the cave-dwellers of Matmata in the south - to ensure cool summers and equable winters. Despite its 2,000-ft altitude, Bulla Regia's summer climate is best described as torrid. The city dates from before the Roman conquest, and reached its peak of prosperity during the golden age when Roman settlers made big money from agricultural exports.

In the basement floors of several luxury villas, fine mosaics with some figures are still in place. Other finds have been removed to the Bardo Museum. Generally, dining and bedroom accommodation was below ground level, while other rooms were on the normal ground floor. Houses in the most affluent residential area have been individually named from their mosaic decorations: Palace of the Hunt, which is the largest and most luxurious, with a subterranean colonnade around a central courtyard; Peacock; Fishing, which possibly was a sanctuary rather than a private house; Amphitrite, who shares a mosaic with Neptune and a number of Cupids.

Public buildings are above ground. There's the usual central grouping of a Forum, Capitol and market-place; several baths, temples and a Theatre. In the 4th century, St Augustine preached in this Theatre, vigorously denouncing the local citizens for their dissolute habits, like spending their money on women. The acoustics are good and performances are given from time to time in spring or summer.

Maktar

About 50 road miles south of Dougga is Maktar. Its location in central Tunisia, commanding the crossing-point of trade routes, gave it a strategic importance for the Numidian kings who controlled this region in Punic times. Even after Julius Caesar's conquest of the Numidians in 46 BC, the city kept a self-governing status. Gradually, over the next 200 years, the Punic traditions faded, and Maktar finally became a full Roman colony around 180 AD. Punic deities likewise switched, and became Roman.

Just like in other cities, Maktar then enjoyed a period of great prosperity which created a major building boom. Most of the archaeological remains date from that period, apart from Christian churches built in the 4th to 6th centuries. A museum and archaeological garden exhibits statues, potteries and inscriptions that have more recently been excavated.

The Great Thermal Baths are among the best preserved in the whole of Africa, with walls that tower 40 feet high around the ground-floor mosaic pavement. Likewise the Forum pavement is completely preserved, and the adjoining triumphal arch of Trajan is in beautiful condition for its age, dated 166 AD.

Elsewhere on the site is the Schola of the Juvenes - a youth centre for sport, gymnastics, swimming and meetings. Curiously, the young men also had a militia and tax-gathering function, and taxes were received here in kind.

Later, the pagan building was converted to Christianity, but its dedication as a church did not save it from the Vandals in the 5th century.

Sbeitla

Still further due south is Sbeitla, neatly located on highway GP 3 which runs from Kairouan to the mountain and desert oases of Gafsa and Tozeur. Hence, on some itineraries, a visit can be included in two-day or three-day safaris to the South.

As a Roman garrison town, intended to block Berber incursions into the fertile lands, Sbeitla had a quiet time in history until 646 AD. In that year, the Byzantine Patriarch Gregory rejected rule from Constantinople, declared UDI and made Sbeitla his capital. But independence was very short-lived. In the following year came the first Arab invasion. Patriarch Gregory went down in defeat. Sbeitla was well and truly looted, and the Arabs went home to Egypt laden with the proceeds. Within twenty years they came back, and stayed.

Entrance to the site is marked by the 3rd-century Diocletian Triumphal Arch, which makes a splendid colour-photo subject with its honey-coloured stone and Corinthian columns. Set against a blue sky, it's a readymade travel poster.

Within the site itself, the Forum area is remarkably well preserved, with a surrounding 13-ft wall. Three temples, mounted on platforms above the Forum, are dedicated to Juno, Jupiter and Minerva. The overall effect is deeply impressive.

Heading out between the temples, you come to a line of Christian monuments - basilica, chapel, and a cathedral with five aisles.

Djerba –
Pause for a friendly gossip
outside one of the principal
mosques of Houmt-Souk

Who's for a camel-ride ?

Nabeul –
A pottery merchant waits
to do business

Folklore night in a resort hotel

9. North to the Coral Coast

Tabarka

Tunisia's 200-mile northern coastline, backed by green forests, low mountains and rolling countryside, has been a late starter in the holiday industry. The region was quite undeveloped except for a relatively modest tourist industry at Tabarka, close to the Algerian border. Now things are changing rapidly, particularly through building of an international-standard airport to bring holidaymakers direct into Tabarka.

Formerly, none of the major British tour operators offered holidays to Tabarka. That was mainly a question of logistics, as the resort was far removed from Monastir, the nearest charter-flight airport served from Britain. Until 1989, the resort could offer only 1500 beds, which mainly were filled by the Italians and French.

Tabarka's current expansion is modelled on the pattern of Port El Kantaoui, designed for year-round holidaymaking. The focus is an up-market Marina with 280-berth capacity - part of a purpose-built complex of 860 acres covering the area known as Larmel, the island of El Morjane, and the seafront facing it.

There's a 27-hole golf course, and all the usual recreational facilities such as watersports and horse-riding. For winter visitors, the complex features a heated swimming pool, ice rink, tennis and squash courts. Other planned amenities include a sea-water and fitness centre with swimming pool, gymnasium, saunas and solarium; and a cultural and entertainment area with casino, summer university and open-air theatre.

Bed capacity is being increased to 10,000 during the next few years. Included in the development is a 400-bed aparthotel, and a range of apartments and luxury villas.

Meanwhile, the sleepy town and fishing port of Tabarka is also changing, with a major renovation programme to help its integration into the new resort complex. Scenically, Tabarka is well endowed. Its natural harbour was first developed by the Carthaginians, and the Romans used it for exports of cork from the forests of Khroumiria, and for grain shipments from the fertile bread basket of the north.

Tabarka's bay is dominated by the island which has been linked to the mainland since 1952 by a French-built causeway. In the 16th century, the Genoese perched a castle on the island peak, and remained there for 200 years even though the Turks held the mainland. The Genoese made good money as middlemen, arranging the ransom of slaves held in Tunis.

For a more reputable source of income, Tabarka has been famous since Carthaginian times as a source of coral. Offshore divers sustain a flourishing industry in coral jewellery made by local craftsmen. As a tourism spin-off, scuba diving has become a popular sport, well supported by young French enthusiasts. Instruction is available through the Tabarka Yachting Club, where equipment can be hired.

The Yacht Club is also the base for deep-sea fishing, under-water photography, varied boat trips, and the organising of deep-sea sport competitions. Spear-fishing is ideal. Uninhabited islands and coastal rocky areas offer total peace for viewing coral beds on the sea floor. The islands are also a haven for lobsters, and a protected colony of Mediterranean seals.

The so-called Coral Festival, held in July and August, is an informal international event covering music, painting, ceramics and the like, with performers and artists mingling with the holidaymakers for cultural exchange and discussion. Outside that period, and until the resort complex is fully developed, nightlife is minimal.

Hills close to Tabarka are densely forested, mainly with cork oak-trees and eucalyptus, well nourished by heavy winter rainfall. The forest and an adjoining area of bushes and shrubs have historically always been rich in game - amply documented by Roman mosaics in Bardo Museum. Modern-day hunters come especially for wild boar, and also for jackal, fox, mongoose and genet. The hunting season goes from the last week of September until the end of March.

Twelve miles south of Tabarka, the principal rendezvous for hunters is the mountain resort of Ain Draham. Located at 2,600-ft altitude, winter snow is not unknown. In summer, the cooler mountain air attracts hikers for marked trails through the forest. Further south on highway GP 17 are the Roman remains of Bulla Regia.

Bizerta

Mileage to Bizerta: Tabarka 90; Tunis 40; Nabeul/Hammamet 80; Sousse 130; Monastir 140; Sfax 210; Gabès 270; Gafsa 265; Tozeur 320; Djerba 360.

Between Taberka and Bizerta, some small beaches are accessible by tracks that lead down from the direct coastal road - MC 51 - that runs parallel to the coast, about 10 miles inland. Otherwise, that coastline is totally innocent of any holiday development.

Bizerta itself is a commercial port with a long history from Punic times onwards. The old harbour, a sanctuary for fishing craft, has a delightful atmosphere, leading the visitor into the well-preserved Medina. It's certainly worth exploring. Bizerta also has some beaches; but the town earns a good living from its seaport activities and has really made no great effort to build up tourism.

A waterway leads into the huge natural harbour formed by the 43 square miles of Lake Bizerta. Well placed for Mediterranean trade and a few centuries as a pirate lair, Bizerta has also played a major part in strategic thinking. Possession of Bizerta was vital during the North African campaigns. Even after Tunisian independence in 1957, the French were reluctant to quit the Bizerta naval base, which they held until 1963.

The Lake of Bizerta has nothing much for visitors, but the adjoining Lake Ichkeul is the most interesting of Tunisia's five National Parks. The protected area includes mountain, lake and swamp habitats for many mammals such as water buffalo, boars, porcupines and otters. Naturalists claim more than 500 plant species. The Ichkeul National Park is winter home for 400,000 birds of many species, and is firmly established on the migration routes between Europe and Africa - south-bound in November, north-bound in March-April. One or two specialist companies operate bird-watching tours that feature the two extremes of Lake Ichkeul and the desert oases of the South.

10. Travellers' Vocabulary

For what it's worth, you could learn the Arabic numerals. However, most of the commercial people with whom holidaymakers come in contact are totally multi-lingual in Arabic and European numbers.

Nearly all Tunisians, particularly in the tourist areas, speak French as a second language, which is obligatory in schools even from primary level. Local kids in holiday resorts begin to learn languages very fast and young, with a constant stream of tourists on whom to practise. Basic English is no problem, and most of them can also make a good showing in German, Swedish or Dutch. Dexterity with languages enables bright and ambitious youngsters to get jobs in hotels or souvenir shops.

To summarise: your time is far better spent in polishing up your French, than in trying to learn the Tunisian brand of Arabic. However, here's a short-list of local words which appear in place-names, etc. They are worth learning, as a sightseeing aid.

Bab a monumental city gate; a door

Bir a well

Bled the countryside

Borj a fort

Chechia the traditional red skull cap worn by men

Chott Large salt-flats, characteristic of the region stretching from the Gulf of Gabès into Algeria

Dar a house, or palace

Djebel mountain

Djemaa a town's principal mosque, for Friday worship

Erg sand dunes

Fondouk a medieval type of caravanserai, where travelling merchants and envoys could stay temporarily and do business

Ghar a cave

Ghorfa vaulted storage chambers for grain, built into the fortified granaries of the Berber south-east

Hadj title given to Moslems who have made the pilgrimage to Mecca

Hammam Turkish-style public bath

Imam an Islamic priest

Jebbah the long white robe with arm-slits, worn by well-to-do city dwellers

Jerid countryside with palm trees

Kasbah the central fortress of an Arab town

Kef cliff

Koubba the dome of a holy man's tomb

Ksar a defensive hilltop granary, characteristic of south-eastern Tunisia

Maghreb meaning 'west', applied to the western countries of North Africa - principally Morocco, Algeria, Tunisia; but also including Mauretania and Libya.

Marabout A local saint, enshrined in a square-shaped domed tomb. The burial place is also called a marabout, and is often a site of local pilgrimage.

Masjid a neighbourhood mosque, usually quite small

Medina a walled Arab town

Medressa an Islamic seminary where students lodge in cells around a courtyard

Menzel the barrel-vaulted farmsteads of Djerba

Mihrab within a mosque, the niche which points the direction of Mecca Minbar pulpit from which the Imam delivers his Friday sermon

Muezzin The priest who calls the faithful to prayer five times daily from a mosque minaret. Today, the call of the muezzin is usually a loudspeaker tape recording played at pre-set times.

Oued French spelling of wadi, a dried-up watercourse

Ras a cape or headland

Ribat a monastic coastal fortress garrisoned by devout Moslems who pledged themselves for martyrdom in the battles against Christianity

Riadh a garden

Sahel the seashore, applied to the central coastal region of Tunisia

Sebkha a salt flat

Souk an Arab market

Tell hill

Tourbet a VIP mausoleum, more prestigious than a marabout

Finally, a few odd words which may come useful:

Choukran means thank you; **Salaam** is greeting; **Kadesh** is how much or how many?; **Naam** is yes; **La** means no.

11. Food and Drink

Hotel dining rooms in Tunisia aim to keep an international clientele happy. So most of the menu choice could appear anywhere in the Mediterranean.

Thanks to Tunisia's century-long connection with France, the cuisine is predominantly French in character. French visitors still heavily outnumber the Germans and the British, and help keep culinary standards in line. A restaurant in Hammamet proclaims 'Hier schmeckt es wie bei Mutter zu Hause,' - just like Mum's cooking - but otherwise it's mainly French cuisine with a Tunisian flavour. Even the local Arabs prefer the long and crusty French loaf.

The principal Tunisian assault on your taste-buds comes from a hot red spice called harissa, made principally from paprika with a touch of salt and garlic. The more vicious varieties can burn the roof off your mouth, but restaurants that cater for visitors normally use a milder version which avoids permament damage and ensures survival for another meal.

When you start an authentic Tunisian meal, a saucer of harissa paste appears on the table along with the bread; and you fill in time until the first course arrives, spreading the harissa like marmalade. Harissa can then re-appear in soups, hors d'oeuvres and main dishes.

Reading the Menu

Among the Tunisian specialities, here are some dishes worth trying:

Octopus salad - slices of cold, cooked octopus, chewy like stewed hose-pipe but more tasty.

Salade Mechouia - tomatoes, onions and peppers grilled over charcoal and served cold with tuna, hard boiled eggs, olives and parsley.

Salade Tunisienne - the main ingredients are hard boiled eggs, tuna fish, chopped-up peppers and tomatoes, with maybe celery and capers.

Chorba - a generic word for 'soup', comes in many guises, but usually heavily laced with harissa.

Brik à l'oeuf - a popular favourite! It consists of a triangular envelope of thin batter or pastry folded around a raw egg. When sealed, the brik is deep-fried in olive oil until the casing is crisp, the egg-white is set and the yolk is still runny. Local etiquette demands that you eat it with your fingers. Knife and fork is for softies. Grasp each end of the hypotenuse and bite into the brik without getting egg-yolk down your T-shirt. You can also have a brik with seafood - such as Brik au Thon with tunny, or Brik fruits de mer - or there are variations with cheese, vegetables or meat. Some restaurants promote their own Brik Maison, giving you the unusual experience of eating a House Brik.

ENTREES STARTERS مفتحات

Salade de Tomates assiette de tomates tomaten salat	2.000	سلاطة طماطم	**tomato's salad** pomodori insalata
Salade Tunisienne salade mixte au thon Tunesischer salat mit thunfisch	2.000	سلاطة تونسية	**tunisian vegetable salad** insalata tunisina
Salade Tabboulé salade tabboulé (beldi) orientalischer salat	2.500	سلاطة تبولي	**oriental salad** insalata orientale
Salade Emira variétés de salades du pays fürstenteller gemischter salat	2.500	صحن الأميرة	**emira salad platter** varietà di insalata
Méchouia au Thon * salade grillée au thon grillsalat mit thunfisch	2.500	سلاطة مشوية بالتن	**grilled salad** insalata alla griglia
Salade de Poulpe * poulpe assaisonnée pulpen salat	3.500	سلاطة أخطبوط	**octopus dress with lemon** polipo condito al limone
Hlalem soupe Tunisienne Tunesische suppe	2.000	حلالم	**Tunisian soup** zuppa Tunisina

Soupe de Poisson aux grains d'orge fischsuppe	2.500	شربة سمك	**fish soup** zuppa di pesce
Brik Capitaine brik aux chevrettes brik mit kl. crevetten	3.000	بريك بالقمبري	**crispy pancake with sm prawns** crespelle fritti al gamberetti
Brik au Thon brik au thon et aux câpres brik mit thunfisch und kapern	2.500	بريك بالتن	**crispy pancacke with tuna-fish** crespelle fritti al tonno
Mini briks "Maison" mini briks "maison" (doigt de Fatma) hausgemachter "brik"	3.000	بريكات «دياري»	**house crispy pancacke** mini crispelle
Omelette Nature	2.000	أوملات طبيعية	
Omelette Andalouse	2.500	أوملات أندلسية	
Ojja aux Merguez ojja aux œufs et aux merguez ojja mit eier und würstchen	3.000	عجة بالمرقاز	**scrambled eggs and sausages** ojja con salsice tunisina

| **Sdir aux Câpres** soupe aux câpres griessuppe mit kapern | 2.000 | سدر بالكبار | **soup with câpres** zuppa con capperi |

Entrées Spéciales/Special Starters/مفتحات خاصـة

Spaghetti Bolognaise	4.000	سباقتي بولوناز	
Makarouna Zina macaroni au thon et aux câpres macaroni mit thunfisch und kapern	4.000	مكرونة زينة	macaroni with tuna-fish and capers macaroni al tonno capperi
Calmar Doré calmar en beignets fritierte kalmares	4.500	منطيق مقلي	**squid fritter** calamari fritti
Cocktail Gondole cocktail de chevrettes kl. crevetten cocktail	6.000	كوكتيل قمبري	**sm. prawns cocktail** cocktail di gamberetti

Assiette de Fruits de Mer * Clovis Moules meeresfrüchte teller	6.000	صحن غلال البحر	**seafood platter** Frutti di Mare
Crevettes en Salade salade aux crevettes crevetten salat	8.000	سلاطة قبري	**praw'ns salad** insalata di gamberetti
Pâtes Marina macaroni aux fruits de mer ou aux chevrettes macaroni mit Kl. crevetten oder meeresfrüchte teller	8.000	مكرونة مارينا	**macaroni with seafood or prawns** macaroni al gamberetti ou frutti di mare

Menus spéciaux, Traiteur et diners de Gala : arrangement et conditions suivant la commande et les désirs du client.
Spécial menu, catering and gala dinners : arrangement and conditions according to the order and the wishes of the client.
Spezialles menu, "Catering" Partie - Service und Gala Abendessen : arrangement und Konditionen nach Ihren Wünschen.

حسب "الضور"
* selon disponibilité
depending on availability

صحن رئيسي على الأقل
un plat de résistance au minimum

Fatima's Fingers - Doigts de Fatima. Another variation of brik, rather like Spring Rolls in Chinese cuisine.

Tajine - a meat, cheese and egg pie, which can be greatly enlivened with harissa peppers, and served hot or cold. Looks like bread pudding gone yellow.

Mermez - mutton stew with broad beans.

Ojja - a messy-looking arrangement of egg scrambled with pieces of Tunisian sausage, potatoes and peppers and with heavy use of harissa. Tastes far better than it looks, and is a good standby for a light lunch.

Couscous - the national dish. It has a ground-base of steamed semolina with an addition of stewed meat or fish, numerous vegetables such as carrots, peas, onions, celery, beans, chick peas, turnips and anything else that comes to hand - all moistened with a spicy sauce.

Kebab - diced lamb or mutton, roasted on skewers over charcoal.

Merguez - a spicey lamb sausage.

Koucha - baked baby lamb, very tender, seasoned with rosemary.

Doulma (dolma) dishes - based on stuffed aubergines or green peppers, with mysterious fillings of minced meat, rice and varied flavourings.

Cheese - There is a locally made blue cheese, patterned on Roquefort, called numidia. Other cheeses - mostly like the white Greek feta - are made from goat or ewe's milk, and are called matur. A French-style Camembert is very good.

Desserts are often very sweet, swimming with sugar syrup, and owe much to Turkish cuisine:

Loukoum - Turkish delight.

Helva - the Middle-East sweet based on sesame seed with nuts.

Baklava - flaky pastry stuffed with nuts and honey.

Begla Mehcheya - dates stuffed with almond paste and sugar, and flavoured with rose water.

Assida - a sweet custard made from hazel nuts, milk and eggs, with chopped nuts as decoration.

Quince jam - often served at breakfast, looks like dried-up chutney.

Choosing a Restaurant

A simple rule of thumb is to avoid going into restaurants which do not have their priced menu displayed outside. This can save some embarrassing moments when you find the final bill is far higher than you expected. You can expect to pay more in restaurants which include a belly-dancer and a three-piece Tunisian band with the evening menu.

For price comparisons, try following the brik à l'oeuf standard. Virtually all Tunisian restaurants include brik à l'oeuf among the starters. In the lowest-cost eatery this item would cost around 20p; in a high-grade establishment, four times as much. You can quickly get a rough guideline to the relative price-scale.

Many restaurants offer a set menu, especially for the lunchtime trade. In the centre of Tunis, for instance, simple restaurants in side streets off the main Avenue Bourguiba offer a decent little lunch for 2 dinars. A typical choice could be a good soup, rich with harissa, a plate of haricot beans, also with harissa sauce, fried liver, fried potatoes and a bottle of Boga lemonade. Note that purely Tunisian restaurants do not serve alcohol.

Fish

With 750 miles of coastline, Tunisia is particularly rich in seafood: red mullet, sea bass, prawns, perch, sole, flounder, hake, grouper, bream, octopus, you-name-it. The lobster season runs from mid-May till late September. There is mass slaughter of tuna-fish in May-June off the Cap Bon coast near Sidi Daoud, where the victims are canned.

Near every harbour there's good choice of fish restaurants, with ethnic lobster-pot decor. Menu prices are often quoted by weight, so-much per hundred grammes (about 4 ounces). Watch that point carefully, or you may be startled to find the cost of your fish is three times higher than expected. When choosing your fish, don't be bashful about asking for a weight and price estimate. It's normally too late to re-weigh the fish after you have eaten it.

The Tunisian fruits

Virtually year-round, Tunisia is a fruitarian's paradise. According to season, here's what to expect:

Oranges and **clementines** - go from October till the end of June. The best oranges are exported.

Dates - are harvested from September, but are available year-round as they are now kept in cold storage. Dates bought in season taste totally different from the boxed fruit sold in Britain at Christmas.

Lemons - right through the year.

Apricots - from mid-April to mid-June.

Plums - in May, June and July.

Grapes - from the beginning of July onwards, and will last through till December.

Apples - which cannot compare in size and appearance with those grown in Europe - are sold from the beginning of June.

Peaches - June till the end of August.

Strawberries - grown in greenhouses - starting in January and going right through till the end of July.

Figs - from June till September.

Sweet melons - grown in greenhouses, start in January and continue for nine months.

Water melons - from May till October.

Pears - from August.

Almonds - available freshly picked in their green shells, are quite different in flavour from the dried-up nuts which reach England's shops. Better pack nutcrackers, unless you have teeth that will crack nuts, rather than vice versa. Orchards of almond trees often alternate with olive groves.

Prickly pear - harvest starts about July and continues through September. When carefully unpeeled to avoid acupuncture, the fruit is quite delicious, tasting something like kiwi fruit. Prickly pear is also the favourite fruit of dromedaries and camels.

The Wine List

Tunisia's vineyards date from Punic times. The original cultivation was described by Magon, the pioneer Carthaginian agronomist whose writings were later used as a textbook by the Romans. After the fall of Carthage, when the Romans colonized Tunisia, cultivation continued to flourish, sustaining Rome's Bacchanalia from the vineyards around Carthage and Cap Bon.

When teetotal Islam took over, the vineyards were not uprooted, but were switched to harvest of table grapes. In more recent centuries, wine production became the preserve of non-Islamic settlers, French or Italian. From the early 19th century, viniculture made considerable progress. During the hundred years of French occupation, a substantial export industry was developed. Since then, with the adoption of modern grape-growing techniques, the industry has aimed for quality rather than high production. Today, Germany is the largest single importer of Tunisian wines.

Vineyards cover an area of 84,000 acres, mostly within a 40-mile radius of ancient Carthage. The industry is split between three sectors - State, cooperative and private - with the cooperative sector accounting for 60% of all Tunisian production. There are 14 cooperative cellars, 14 State-owned and 10 private. The grape harvest begins at the end of August, and continues for four or five weeks. Just over half the crop is for wine production, the remainder for table use.

The Tunisian wines - red, white and rosé - are quite acceptable, though with high alcohol content, upwards of 12°. If you insist on imported French, then the prices will shatter you. On a typical wine-list, French champagne costs £60 a bottle, while the local Vin Mousseux costs £4.50. Otherwise, even in a first-class restaurant, Tunisian wines are modestly priced mainly in the range of £1.50 to £3 a bottle.

Here are some names worth trying:

Gris de Tunisie - a rosé wine from the hills of the Mornag region.

Magon - named after the Carthaginian agronomist - is a quality red wine, cultivated on chalk hills of the Tebourba region, west of Tunis.

Muscat Sec de Kelibia - a dry white of guaranteed vintage from Kelibia, near the northern tip of Cap Bon. (There is also a Muscat, made from the Muscat grape, similar to a sweet white port).

Sidi Raïs - a rosé wine from Takelsa, in the Cap Bon area.

Coteaux de Carthage - superior quality red wines from hillsides near Tunis which were originally planted in Punic times.

Château Mornag - a rosé wine from the Mornag area, just outside Tunis.

Château Khanguet - a red vintage 'Sidi Salem' from the Khanguet region.

Blanc de Blanc - a white wine from the Tebourba area.

Domaine de St. Josef - red, white and rosé wines produced by the monks of Thibar Monastery.

For something stronger, the two local spirits to sample are boukha and thibarine.

Thibarine - a dark liqueur made from dates. For this good work, thank the White Fathers of Thibar Monastery, who developed this very successful after-dinner liqueur. It smells like cough mixture, but glows smoothly like a Drambuie.

Boukha - distilled from figs, this firewater burns with a blue flame and is best rinsed down with Coca-Cola. Taken neat, it's rather like being shot in the throat.

The principal local beer is called Celtia, costing about 50p a bottle, hotel-price. It's a light lager type, with good flavour.

Non-alcoholic drinks

Most holidaymakers are nervous about drinking the local tap water laced with chlorine. If you want to play safe with bottled mineral water, try Ain Garci or Ain Oktor, which are gassy; Safia or Ain Melliti, which are still and without taste.

Kintonic is the local tonic. Apla is a non-alcoholic cider.

If you want a simple bottle of sweet and fizzy lemonade, ask for Boga. In the unlikely event that the waiter says 'Boga off!' try asking for Fanta or Coca-Cola instead. Local connoisseurs say that Boga is very pleasant when mixed with wine.

During the appropriate seasons, vendors offer a range of fresh fruit squashes made with a blender. Quite apart from the obvious glass of newly-squeezed orange juice, it's worth sampling the more exotic thirst-quenchers. Try pear juice with strawberries, for instance. Delicious!

English-type tea with milk is best avoided. However, at buffet-style breakfasts you could experiment with the hotel-supplied tea bags, and see how it tastes. Otherwise, the Tunisian speciality is heavily-sugared tea served in glasses, with fresh mint floating. As the drink cools, local wasps land on the mint-leaves - aircraft carriers in miniature - and help themselves to the sweet liquid. If you are anti-wasp, use a saucer as a lid. You can ask for your tea without sugar, but the message often fails to click.

Breakfast coffee in hotels is usually French style, or Nescafé. If a shopkeeper invites you to have a cup of coffee, it will almost certainly be Turkish: a tiny cup, thick with coffee grounds and ready sugared.

12. What to Buy

Shopping for local handicrafts is part of a Tunisian holiday. In the resorts, tourist shops stay open till late evening, mostly seven days a week throughout the season. Shop-gazing becomes part of the nightlife. The larger hotel developments feature their own bazaar areas, packed with concessionaires. Drifting through their shops can help you get a feel on price levels.

Don't rush into buying during the first days of a holiday. Comparison shopping is part of the game, especially in a land where price tickets are often just the starting point for a good old-fashioned haggle. When shopkeepers see that you're not going to pay their asking price, then you'll usually find their quotes become more flexible. Show some mild interest in an item - then shock at the price - begin to walk out, saying you'll try elsewhere . . . If the price is negotiable, it will start crumbling. After a few times, you'll master the art. However, don't start serious bargaining unless you are really interested in buying. It's not fair on the shopkeeper to waste his time, just for the fun of it.

Around the hotels, numerous itinerant vendors try to sell you everything from oranges to carpets. If you don't want to buy or look, just ignore them. If they start to follow you, don't worry. They'll soon realise that you are a lost cause, and will walk away to accost the next potential victim.

When you're wandering through the souks, he or she who hesitates is grabbed. If a salesman offers you a tempting hundred camels for your wife or daughter, it's merely an attention-catching device to lure you into buying a souvenir ash-tray. The hustling by shopkeepers in the medinas is all part of the Tunisian way of life. Don't let it bother you. If you don't want to talk, just walk on, and the hustler will soon tire. Don't let the persistent sales pressure spoil your holiday!

Haggling is even more part of the game in the souks, where starting prices are just plucked out of the sky, depending how the shopkeeper guesses your banknote potential. He starts high, you offer rock bottom, and hopefully you'll settle somewhere in between, at a price satisfactory to both. Maybe you'll end at around half their asking price, but patience is needed.

ONAT

Best policy is to visit an ONAT store, to get a preliminary idea of price levels. The initials stand for Office Nationale d'Artisanat Tunisien - stores operated by the State-owned National Handicraft Office. This splendid organization aims to preserve handicraft standards, and is deeply involved in the training of youngsters in authentic designs and techniques. The social importance of encouraging the labour-intensive crafts is obvious in a country with fast-expanding population. An estimated 120,000 craft workers are spread around the country, and 45,000 hand weavers.

At ONAT stores, you can get an overall view of all the top-quality handicraft products. Everything is totally fixed price. There is not the slightest pressure to buy, as the staff are working on proper salaries, no commission. In contrast to so many private-sector shops, you will not be mauled and pestered.

Look around and get a clear idea of what is a reasonable price. It's then a challenge to your bargaining skills to get private-sector prices down to the levels that you find in ONAT shops. In fact, a determined haggler can even do better than ONAT prices, which are not necessarily at the cheapest level. The ONAT slogan is: 'A high quality tradition at a fair price.'

Where to find ONAT? There are two superb branches in Tunis - on the main Avenue Mohamed V, and close to the Tourist Information Office; two at Nabeul; and one at each of the other principal resorts - Port El Kantaoui, Monastir, Kairouan, Gabès, Zarzis and Houmt Souk (Djerba).

If purchases total more than 50 dinars, ONAT shops give 10% discount when payment is made with hard currency or traveller cheques; or 5% reduction if paid with well-known credit cards such as American Express, Diners, Visa, Eurocard, Mastercard or Access. Well worth considering, if you're buying something major, like a carpet!

Buying a carpet

In Tunisia, the making of rugs and carpets follows a long-established tradition. In the 9th century, Kairouan produced sumptuous carpets which the Aghlabite princes sent in payment of royalties to Bagdad. In the 14th century, Ahmed Ibn Makki, who was then master of Tripoli and Djerba, concluded a treaty with Venice for the free export of Tunisian carpets. In the 15th century, the King of Naples ordered silk materials and woollen carpets from Tunis, to furnish his palaces.

The pure-wool Kairouan knot-stitch carpet varies according to the number of knots per square metre - ranging from 10,000 to 250,000 knots. Those of 250,000 knots are generally of silk, but can be wool. The knot-pile decorated woven carpets are Berber in origin (Mergoum, Klim, tapestries of Gafsa). All Tunisian carpets and weavings are entirely hand-made, and are subject to quality control. They are stamped with the official National Handicrafts seal. This guarantees the quality of the materials used, as well as the weaving process.

All woollen carpets are carefully cleaned of all impurities, and moth-proofed. The weft is wear-resistant twisted cotton. Colours are solid, and are resistant to air, light and water.

Sewn on the back of every carpet is a certificate, showing the grade and origin, its exact size - length, width, and how many square metres - the material of which it is made, and the weight in kilos. Also shown is the so-called 'texture', like 20 X 20.

Prices in ONAT stores are established according to a tariff fixed by the National Handicrafts Office itself, based on so-much per square metre for superior quality and first quality. Thus, prices are identical whether you buy in Kairouan, Tunis or wherever. Carpets stamped 2nd choice are subject to a 20% or 30% reduction compared with 1st quality.

The certificate shows figures like 10 X 10, or 20 by 20. The higher the figure, the higher the quality. Thus, 30 by 30 will be of higher price and quality than 20 by 20. Imagine a square measuring 10 cms by 10 cms (about four inches square). 30 by 30 means that, within that area, there are thirty lines of 30 knots. By multiplying out, 30 by 30 in a square of 10 cms would end as 90,000 knots per square metre, which is another way of expressing the texture. A 50 by 50 silk carpet has a quarter-million knots per square metre, which explains their much higher price.

Obviously, price also depends on the material used: wool, imported wool or silk. LST stands for Laine Supérieure de Tunisie - home-grown wool. Prices are worked out mathematically, and you get an exact quotation to the nearest millime. If you are seriously in the market for a carpet, it's worth taking a pocket calculator with you.

You may be able to find a list of 'indication prices', published by the Ministry of Tourism and of Artisanat, giving the suggested prices in dinars per square metre of different rugs in different qualities.

Whether you buy in the ONAT store or not, their prices give you a good guideline on what to pay for a carpet, bearing in mind the material, quality and texture. Sometimes you can negotiate a better deal from private-sector shops. They may keep close to ONAT prices, but will also offer port payé (carriage paid), in order to close the deal.

Carpets bought by British visitors are subject to Customs Duty and VAT on the total price paid, plus the cost of stamps, insurance and handling charges. Carriage will be payable from the UK entry port to your home. Port Payé on the receipt means carriage paid to the port of entry, not the home address. Anything you're told to the contrary by sales people should be disregarded.

Handicrafts worth buying

Here's a brief list of possible purchases which can be an authentic reminder of Tunisia:

Woven products made from palm fronds, sheep's wool, camel and goat hair.

Blankets, in traditional patterns.

Berber woollen shawls called bakhnoug, blue or red, embroidered with geometric designs.

Necklaces, with your name in Arabic; in silver, gold plate or solid gold.

Jewellery: silver and gold, enamel and filigree work. For specialized items, production is based in specific centres

- Tunis for gold, with or without the use of precious stones,

- Nabeul and Sfax for peasant women's silver jewelry,

- Moknine for solid silver jewelry,

- Monastir, Mahdia and Sousse for solid gold and silver jewelry,

- Djerba for solid silver and filigree silver ware.

Pottery: pots, plates, vases etc, hand-painted in local designs. The principal centres are Nabeul, Djerba and Moknine.

Hand-painted tiles: excellent choice at Nabeul.

Copperware: ashtrays, traditional utensils, and platters and trays of various sizes, all hand tooled, some with inlaid patterns of silver or brass. Although widespread, copperware is a speciality of Tunis and Kairouan.

Embroidered kaftans, and other robes in silk or wool.

Leather goods: leather jackets, bags, belts, purses, wallets, pouffes etc.

Birdcages: highly ornamental in the blue and white Sidi Bou Said designs. With a few basic alterations, they can be adapted as hanging flower holders, or even as light fixtures.

Rushwork baskets.

Perfumes.

Stuffed toy animals, who are about 90% camels.

Tom-tom drums and flutes and various stringed instruments. Many of the traditional wooden musical instruments are produced at Kelibia.

For keen cooks, spices are worth taking home. Saffron costs a fraction of the English price. Other spices and condiments can be equally cheap. Also on offer at any weekly market are sacks of caraway, coriander and cumin seeds; aniseed, cinnamon, turmeric, rosemary, ginger, cloves and bay leaves. Open-air spice markets also give super colour shots for your camera.

Traditional Market Days

Friday - Jebeniana; Midoun; Thala; Zarzis; Jemmal; Nabeul; Testour; Ksour Essaf; Oeslatia; Sfax; Mateur; Tabarka; Zaghouan; Mahdia

Saturday - Ben Gardane; El Alia; El Fahs; Thibar

Sunday - El Djem; Enfidaville; Hamman-Lif; Ksar Hellal; Sousse; Fernana; Sfax

Monday - Ain Draham; Kairouan; Maharès; Mareth; Chebba Houmt Souk; Makthar; Tataouine

Tuesday - Béja; Haffouz; Kasserine; Menzel Témime; El Hajeb; Ghardimaou; Krib; Souk Sebet; Ksar Hellal

Wednesday - Jendouba; Nefta; Sers; Sbeitla; Moknine

Thursday - Douz; Djerba; Téboursouk; Gafsa; Bousalem; Menzel Bouzelfa.

13. Looking at the Past

History and Architecture

Over 2,000 years have passed since Hannibal's army crossed the Alps with a baggage-train of elephants. His men had come from North Africa and through Spain to attack their old foes, the Romans, from the north. That was just one incident of the Punic Wars. But much later travellers to Tunisia were reminded of it when they tried to recapture an idea of ancient Carthage. For there, on the site of the Imperial city, an Arab village huddled among the stables that formerly housed those famous elephants.

The Carthaginian empire was the first of the seven civilizations that have ruled Tunisia, each leaving its distinctive mark on the country's history and architecture. Repeated invasions have shattered the more ancient cities, but enough remains to transform Tunisia into an architectural student's paradise.

Carthage itself was founded in 814 BC by the Phoenicians - the sea-traders from the Levant who flourished throughout the Mediterranean and who even bartered purple cloth for Cornwall's tin. Today, in southern Tunisia, similar cloth is still being produced by descendants of dyers who - according to Pliny - rivalled Tyre for the beauty of their purple. Exploring the remains of the Punic city of Kerkouan, on the Cap Bon coast north of Nabeul, you can inspect the industrial site where Phoenician settlers made their purple dye from shell-fish.

As the Punic trading empire expanded, it clashed more and more with Rome. But, even after the second Punic War, when Hannibal was defeated, Carthaginian prosperity continued to boom.

At that time, the Roman statesmen Cato was member of a deputation which visited Carthage. Greatly alarmed at the city's wealth and undiminished power, he conducted a 40-year campaign to have Carthage eliminated. Whatever the subject that was being discussed in the Senate, he ended his every speech by saying 'In addition, I think Carthage must be destroyed' - 'Delenda est Carthago'. He didn't live long enough to see it happen. But in 146 BC, only four years after Cato's death, the Romans conquered Carthage, and the great mercantile city of Carthage was sacked, put to the flames and levelled. All that has survived today are a few drains, half a dozen gigantic cisterns, a cemetery and an excavated housing development.

But soon the Romans were back, sent by Julius Caesar to rebuild the city bigger and better. The grandeur of Carthage once again began to rival that of Rome. Art, science and religion flourished.

The Romans were much more than

traders. They were colonizers, too. Spreading into the interior, they built temples, theatres, palaces, baths and villas. During that period, Tunisia became a wealthy granary of Rome. Villa remains are found even in the most deserted countryside. In the Bardo Museum of Tunis, superb mosaics give a vivid impression of the Roman life-style: hunting scenes, feasting and drinking, sport and entertainment.

The Romans were also great civic engineers. Faced with the water problem presented by a city of 700,000 inhabitants, they built a magnificent aqueduct that carried 6,000,000 gallons of water daily into Carthage from hills eighty miles away. Most of the aqueduct is still there, though water no longer flows. Instead, for long centuries after the engineering collapsed, the few remaining villagers laboriously toiled with buckets from a well, though sometimes with the help of ox-power.

During latter stages of Roman occupation, Christianity was spreading through the Empire. The need arose for a new style of building, suitable for Christian worship. The basilica form, with its central nave and two side aisles produced by the interior colonnade, proved to be the most adaptable. During the 4th and 5th centuries many were erected in Tunisia.

But the Roman Empire was crumbling. In 439 AD the Vandals swept in, and Carthage was ravaged again. There followed a hundred years of anarchy, only ended when the Byzantines drove out the barbarians in 535. Main speciality of the Vandal rule was a talent for destruction. They are blamed for castrating Roman statues, and also knocking off their noses. It

was a deliberate action to symbolize triumph over their impotent enemies.

With the Byzantines came a fresh architectural influence. Their stay, however, was relatively short. They were soldiers rather than colonizers, more concerned in reducing the fading towns to the defensible minimum.

Their contribution to the Tunisian scene lay mainly in the realm of fortifications. As Christians, though, they brought the Byzantine style of church, with its characteristic dome imported from the Orient.

Next it was the turn of the Arabs. Swarming across the empty lands under the banner of triumphant Islam, Okba ben Wafi, conqueror of Africa, pitched his camp at the head of a desolate plateau. There he began to build his first great African mosque. Within forty years of the Prophet's death, the Holy City of Kairouan was already under construction. As a capital and a place of pilgrimage, Kairouan expanded rapidly with building of housing, craft workshops and trading areas; more mosques for the increased population, and fortifications.

The genius of the Arab world was in letting the buildings of the past fall apart, and then carting off any bits that might come in handy. Over the centuries, the stone quarry that was Carthage was exploited to the full. Even the poorest of tenement houses in Tunis today possess their capitalled columns and marble stairways, whilst carved inscriptions to Jupiter make excellent doorsteps. But, in truth, the Arabs were not the only stone-robbers; for even the cathedrals of Genoa and Pisa were built from Carthage marble.

Islamic architecture excels in

geometric decoration. As precaution against idolatry, the Koran forbids the making of any graven image or the likeness of anything in heaven or earth. Following this guideline, craftsmen concentrated on purely formal design, rich in colour, carving and intricate schemes of light and shade. The contrast with Roman exuberance could not be more extreme.

Over the centuries, the arabesque with its fantastic wealth of detail has become a sterile form. Into the 20th century, Tunisian stone-masons and tile-painters continue their production of stylized ornament, copying traditional themes handed down over the generations.

Meanwhile, the pattern of the towns was established. During the week, attendance for the five-times-daily prayers would be in small neighbourhood mosques. But on Fridays the faithful flocked to the city's Great Mosque - the principal Friday mosque where the week's big sermon is delivered. Grouped close to the Friday mosque were the main religion-based institutions - a theological school, charitable foundations, soup kitchen and lodgings for travellers. With the Islamic call for ritual cleanliness before prayer, a major public bath - hammam - would be in close proximity.

Around this city focal-point, covered bazaars and workshops developed. Merchants established themselves along the main alleys that led from city entrance-gates to the Great Mosque. In side-alleys were concentrated the principal craft-workers, each tightly grouped together. Customers who wanted footwear would go direct to the slipper-makers' bazaar, and choose from the output of several dozen workshops. Closest to the

Great Mosque would be the more noble trades: booksellers, perfumers, jewellers. Furthest away, on the city outskirts, were banished the noisier and smellier trades: metal-bashers, tanners and dyers.

All this basic layout survives into the 20th-century walled medinas of Tunis, Sousse and Sfax, with housing spread haphazard in a maze of winding streets and culs-de-sac. These residential dead ends - often entered through semi-dark vaulted passages - are regarded as private, not to be used by anyone who doesn't live there. At the city's highest point, overlooking the medina, a Kasbah stronghold completes the urban system. To a European visitor, accustomed to a modified chess-board of city blocks, the overall scheme seems chaotic. But the Islamic city follows a medieval logic which works well - even to the extent of retaining a pedestrianized precinct, safe from motor cars.

The next two foreign occupiers - Spanish and then Turkish - had a comparatively small influence on Tunisian architecture. The 16th-century Spaniards were content with building or upgrading castles along the coast, leaving the interior to take care of itself. Before long they were driven out by the Turks, who installed a pasha to rule.

The Turkish government had only one concern - the collection of tribute for the sultan's coffers. Under the crushing burden of taxation, the country steadily decayed. The state revenues were balanced only by revenue from piracy, which politely was called privateering. After three centuries of Ottoman rule, the former granary of Rome had less than one tenth of its cultivable land still under the plough. In this condition of anarchy, it is hardly surprising that the Turks left scanty mark on the Tunisian scene. All they contributed were a few Turkish-style mosques and the vast palace of the Beys, whose harem has since been converted into the Bardo archaeological museum.

From 1881 until 1956, Tunisia was a French Protectorate. The general policy was to build European quarters outside the massive walls of the ancient towns, and to leave the Tunisians to themselves. The expatriate French architecture has little that is remarkable: maybe a boulevard or two, with cafés, restaurants and the usual public buildings in French provincial style. Otherwise, blocks of apartments line straight roads. Elsewhere, pseudo-Moorish with cheap stucco was the rule.

Meanwhile, what about the original residents of Tunisia, the Berbers? Herodotus - the 'Father of History' - wrote in the fifth century BC that some of the inhabitants lived in caves. The first three occupations - Punic, Roman and Byzantine - left them untouched. Later, however, they were converted to Islam and mostly became Arabised.

Nowadays, the pure Berber survives in only a few districts - notably in the south. On the island of Djerba, for instance, they live in fortified farmhouses, cuboid or barrel-vaulted in design.

Most amazing of all, in this 20th century AD, is that Berbers of the Matmata district are still living in the style of caves that Herodotus described. The region offers all forms of troglodyte architecture.

Who's Who

Aghlabites Arab rulers of Tunisia, 800-909 AD - a Golden Age in the country's history. The Aghlabites also conquered Sicily, and expanded their rule from Constantine in Algeria to Tripoli in Libya.

Augustus Roman emperor, mainly responsible for rebuilding of Carthage from 29 BC.

Barbarossa Turkish-backed privateer - more often described as a pirate - who captured Tunisia's main cities in 1534. Most of his fleet was sunk by the Spaniards under Charles V in the following year.

Beni Hilali A savage Arabian tribe who swept through Tunisia in the 11th century, destroying town and countryside.

Bourguiba, Habib Leader of Tunisian independence, and first President of the Republic.

Cato Roman statesman, 234-149 BC, who constantly urged his fellow senators to undertake a Third Punic War and destroy Carthage.

Dido A fugitive princess from Tyre, who became the reputed founder of Carthage.

Draghut A Turkish captain of Greek origin, born around 1500. He established a pirate base on Djerba, from where he preyed on sea traffic through the Sicilian narrows.

Fatimites Named after Fatima, daughter of the prophet Mohammed, the Fatimites were a dynasty who ruled Tunisia 909-972. They established Mahdia as their capital. Led by El Moez, they conquered Egypt in 969 and then transferred their power centre to Cairo.

Genseric Leader of the Vandals, who

conquered Tunisia in 439 AD.

Hafsites A dynasty founded by Abu Zakaria, the son of Sheikh Abu Hafs, holding power from 1236 to 1574. They established Tunis as their capital, which in turn gave the country its name.

Hamilcar Barca Carthaginian leader who somewhat drastically quelled a revolt in 237 BC by crushing 40,000 men to death by elephants.

Hannibal Carthaginian general, son of Hamilcar Barca, whose niche in history is assured by his exploit of invading Italy over the Alps, with a baggage-train of elephants.

Homer Greek poet, author of *The Odyssey* in which Odysseus - among his many adventures - visited what is identified as the Lotus Island of Djerba

Hussein Ben Ali In 1705 he proclaimed himself Bey of Tunis, setting up the hereditary Husseinite dynasty - the Rule of the Beys, which survived until the monarchy was abolished in 1957.

Mago A 6th-century BC Carthaginian agronomist whose treatise on agriculture was sent to Rome for translation, after the destruction of Carthage. It became a standard work of reference, especially for cultivation of grapes and olives.

Odysseus Legendary hero of Homer's *Odyssey*. Sailed on a prolonged voyage that included a lotus-eating interlude on the island of Djerba, followed by a journey north along the Tunisian coast to the lagoons and fertile lowlands of Tunis.

Okbaa Ibn Nafaa A disciple of the Prophet Mohammed, he founded the city of Kairouan in 671 AD.

Scipio Roman general who captured Carthage in 146 BC, and razed it to the ground.

Vandals A destructive tribe who conquered Tunisia around the year 439, and stayed until their defeat by the Byzantines in 533 AD.

Zine El Abidine Ben Ali Replaced Habib Bouguiba as President of Tunisia in a bloodless coup on 7 November 1987.

Dates in Tunisian History

B.C.

1100 Phoenicians establish the settlement of Utica.

814 Founding of Carthage by Queen Didon of Tyre. The city rapidly develops, to rival Rome.

264-241 First Punic War. Carthaginians forced to withdraw from Sicily.

219-201 Second Punic War.

218 Hannibal invades Italy with his elephants.

205 Romans drive the Carthaginians out of Spain.

202 Hannibal defeated by Scipio at Zama.

149-146 Third Punic War.

146 Romans, led by Scipio Aemilian, destroy Carthage.

47-46 Julius Caesar campaigns in Africa. Africa becomes a Roman province.

44-39 Resettlement of Carthage.

A.D.

1st and 2nd centuries - great prosperity, with Tunisia as the granary of Rome.

312 Christianity becomes the official religion.

439 Vandals - a German tribe - sack Carthage, and then continue an occupation lasting a hundred years.

533 Collapse of the Vandal Kingdom.

534 Tunisia absorbed into the Byzantine Empire, under Emperor Justinian.

647-700 Arab conquest. Islam replaces Christianity.

670 Kairouan founded by Okbaa Ibn Nafaa.

800-909 The Aghlabites, who make Kairouan their capital, conquer Sicily in 835 and extend their rule from Constantine in Algeria to Tripoli in the East.

909-973 Dynasty of the Fatimides, ruling from Mahdia.

973 Caliph Al Moizz invades Egypt and makes Cairo his capital.

973-1041 Rule of the Zirides, a Berber dynasty.

1041-1222 The Beni Hilali invasion completes the Arabization of the country, but with massive destruction.

1228-1574 A governor declares the independence of Tunisia from the Caliph Almohade and founds the dynasty of the Hafsides, with Tunis as the capital.

1534-1535 Tunis besieged by the pirate Barbarossa.

1535-1574 Spanish protectorate, following the conquest of Tunis by the Emperor Charles V.

1574 Tunisia becomes a Turkish province - part of the Ottoman Empire, with local Turkish rulers.

1705 Hussein Ben Ali seizes power as the Bey of Tunis. The rule of the Beys continues until 1957.

1869 An international commission controls Tunisia's finances, and causes France to intervene in Tunisia's internal affairs.

1881 On a pretext, French troops from Algeria invade Tunisia. France compels the Bey to sign the Treaty of Bardo, which gives France control of Tunisian defence and foreign affairs.

1883 The Convention of La Marsa gives France the right to initiate internal reforms. Following this Convention, a considerable number of French people settle in Tunisia.

1920 Beginnings of a Tunisian nationalist movement, with formation of the Constitutional Liberal Party, or Destour, calling for an elected assembly and a responsible Tunisian government.

1934 Young intellectuals in the Destour break with the old guard and form the Neo-Destour Party under leadership of Habib Bourguiba.

1938 Bourguiba and his companions imprisoned.

1942-43 The North Africa campaign of World War 11 sways back and forth, with final defeat of the Germans.

1945 Bourguiba leaves Tunisia secretly, and launches an international campaign to get support for Tunisian independence.

1956 France recognizes Tunisian independence, and Bourguiba becomes Prime Minister.

1957 Abolition of the monarchy, proclamation of the republic, and Bourguiba is chosen to be President.

1987 Bourguiba deposed, and replaced as President by Zine El Abidine Ben Ali.

14. Modern Tunisia – Facts and Figures

Population Approx 8 million, of whom 1.4 million live in the city and suburbs of Tunis, the capital. Over 50% of the population is under 20 years' old. Rate of increase is 2.6%.

Geography Tunisia's surface area of 48,000 square miles is bounded by the Mediterranean on the north and east; Algeria on the west; Libya and the Sahara on the south. The Saharan territory extends to about 21,500 square miles. A twin mountain chain - the Atlas of the Tell, and the Saharan Atlas - converges in the north east, at Cape Bon. Between the mountain chains and along the coastlines are fertile plains; in the centre, steppelands; in the south, a pre-desert area of salt-flats and luxuriant oases.

Religion 98% of the population is Muslim. Minority religions are Jewish, Catholic, Protestant and Greek Orthodox.

Labour force 35% work in agriculture; 22% industry; 11% in service sectors.

Agriculture About 20% of the gross national product is derived from agriculture and fishing. Sheep and poultry are Tunisia's most important livestock.

Exports The principal exports are textiles, petroleum and natural gas, phosphates, olive oil, sea-food and dates.

Administration Tunisia is a republic, in which the government is responsible both to the President and the National Assembly. The country is divided into 23 'guvernorats', sub-divided into 212 'delegations'.

Tourism Is now Tunisia's most important currency earner, catering for 2 million visitors, who stay in some 450 establishments with capacity of 110,000 beds. This will rise to 125,000 beds by 1991.

The Young

Over 50% of Tunisia's inhabitants are below the age of 20.

Education was made compulsory just after independence. Primary schools were established, even in the most remote areas of the country. The children start school at age six, for six years of primary schooling. First the children are taught in Arabic. From the age of eight they start to learn French; then English from age fourteen.

Secondary education continues for periods of 7, 6 or 3 years, depending on whether children are selected for an academic, technical or trade-school type of education.

Six Tunisian universities include 68 institutions for higher education and scientific research. Student numbers have risen to about 44,000, with another 12,000 studying abroad.

Tunisians are called at age 20 for one year of military service.

Politics

On 7 November 1987, President Bourguiba was succeeded by Zine Ben Ali, in a bloodless coup. The final overthrow of Bourguiba came because he was becoming increasingly senile and unable to make firm decisions. There were several changes of prime minister during Bourguiba's final months of office.

The new President is very popular, and the transfer of power went through smoothly. Zine El Abidine Ben Ali is a highly decisive and hard-working character, who is well-liked for his attention to complaints and petitions. He was born in Hamam-Sousse, and members of the President's family still live in the town. The President also has a residence near Port El Kantaoui, where he comes occasionally to stay.

From the early 60's until the early 80's, Tunisia was a one-party state, ruled by the Neo-Destour - now called RCD (Democratic Constitutional Rally). Today there are five other legal political parties: Tunisian Communist Party (PCT); Movement of Democratic Socialists (MDS); Popular Unity Party (PUP); Social Party for Progress (PSP); and Progressist Socialist Rally (RSP).

The basic policies originated by the Neo-Destour are being pursued, with some modernization or updating. There is movement towards privatization.

Islam

In its adherence to Islam, Tunisia takes a middle-of-the-road attitude - not so fundamentalist as Saudi Arabia, Libya or Morocco; but much less secular-minded compared with Turkey. During Ramadan, the daytime fasting, non-drinking of liquids, and non-smoking find adherence in public, but a more relaxed attitude in private. During the early part of Bourguiba's presidency, he tried to virtually abolish the observance of Ramadan. But he soon retreated from that position.

Meanwhile, part of the policy of the new government aims to go some way towards appeasing the demands of Islamic fundamentalists. There is a call to prayer five times daily on television.

Tourism

With the acknowledged high importance of the tourism sector -now the country's leading currency earner - great stress is placed on training the new generation of hotel employees. There are splendid catering schools in Sousse-Nord and at Skanès-Plage.

During Tunisia's 7th Five-year Plan, 1986-1991, the Tunisian government is investing £520 million in the tourism sector - on the renovation of hotels, purchase of tourist transport, establishment of golf courses in Tunis, Tabarka, Hammamet and Djerba, and in building of casinos and conference centres. The target is to increase hotel bed capacity by 5,000 beds a year, to reach at least 125,000 by 1991.

A Guide to Price Levels

Like so many countries around the world, Tunisia has the persistent problem of inflation, even higher than Britain's. So how does this affect visitors, and their outgoings on holiday expenses: for food, drink, sightseeing and entertainment?

Current financial policy is to adjust exchange rates in line with relative inflation. If the gap between British and Tunisian annual inflation rates is running at 7%, you can expect a roughly parallel difference on exchange rates. Thus, prices remain reasonably stable from year to year in terms of hard currency. As a basic guideline, public transport, local products and services are cheap compared with most European holiday destinations. But, because of high taxation on imports, virtually all foreign goods are very expensive or difficult to find.

To give an idea on what to expect, here are some typical holiday-price figures for 1990.

Travel-agency Excursions

Half-day coach sightseeing tours £6; full day with lunch, £13; full day longer-distance Safari to the South £20 including lunch; two-day Safari £38-£50, depending on the overnight hotel. Evening folklore show with transport, Tunisian meal and unlimited wine, £10.

Eating Out

Depending on grade of restaurant, a light set lunch costs about £2 in a modest establishment. Sample menu prices: Salad 50p; octopus or squid salad £1; soup 35p; brik à l'oeuf 20p; cheese omelette 60p; lamb couscous £1.35; fish couscous £1.60; mixed grill £1.80; grilled lamb cutlets, £1.35.

Menu prices in a 1st-class restaurant: Tunisian Salad £1.50; soup £1.30; brik with seafood £2; omelette £1.35; fish couscous £4. Wines £2 to £3 a bottle. Tunisian sparkling wine £6; French champagne £60 - you have been warned!

Refreshments

In an average café or 2-star hotel: Coke or Pepsi 25p; Celtia beer 40p; bottle of Safia mineral water 30p; mint tea or Turkish coffee 16p; tea with milk 27p; freshly-squeezed orange juice 40p; Tunisian aperitifs 40p; regular whiskies £1.50. At a stand-up cafeteria, those soft-drink prices could be halved!

Top-grade restaurant or bar: soft drinks 50p; beer 90p; mineral water 60p; aperitifs £1.35; Boukha or Thibarine £1.20; regular Scotch £2.35; de luxe Scotch £3.35.

Market Fruit

Prices *per kilo* in the market: honeydew melons 85p; water-melons 28p; derelict-looking apples 50p; apricots 33p; tomatoes 33p; peaches 60p; strawberries 40p; new-harvest almonds in their shells 20p.

Transport Hire

Bicycles £2 or £3 a day; camels or horses £3 an hour; motor-bikes with pillion £10 half day, £13.50 whole day; Renault 4F or 2-door Citroen LNA £10 per day plus 9p per km; Renault 9 £12 per day plus 11p per km. Petrol costs £1.50 per Imperial gallon.

15. Travel Tips and Information

Addresses in Britain

Tunisian National Tourist Office, 7a Stafford Street, London W1X 4EQ. Tel: 01-499 2234. Telex: 261368.

Tunisian Embassy, 29 Prince's Gate, London SW7. Tel: 01-584 8117. Open Mon-Thur 9.30 - 17.00 hrs. Fri 9.30 - 16.00 hrs.
Tunis Air, 24 Sackville Street, London W1X 1DE. Tel: 01-734 7644/5 Reservations (open Mon-Fri 9.30 - 17.00 hrs. Sat 10.00 - 12.00 hrs). Tel: 01-759 2311 Flight Enquiries. Telex: 892605 TUNAIR G.

Addresses in USA

Tunisian National Tourist Office, Tunisian Embassy - Tourism Division, 1515 Massachusetts Ave. NW, Washington, DC 20005.

Addresses in Tunisia

American Consulate, 144 Avenue de la Liberté, Tunis. Tel: 232566.

British Consulate, 5 Place de la Victoire, Tunis. Tel: 245100.

Canadian Consulate, 3 Rue Didon, Tunis. Tel: 286577.

Algerian Consulate, 136 Avenue de la Liberté, Tunis. Tel: 280082.

Libyan Consulate, 48 Rue 1 Juin, Tunis. Tel: 283936.

Moroccan Consulate, 39 Rue 1 Juin, Tunis. Tel: 288063.

Getting there

The national airline, Tunis Air, operates scheduled services direct from London Heathrow to Tunis and Monastir. Otherwise, most holidaymakers travel by tour-operator charter flights - mainly to Monastir, which serves the principal coastal resorts; otherwise to Tunis, Sfax or Djerba.

Surface routes - by land to Marseilles, Genoa, Naples or Palermo, and thence by ferry - are feasible only if you have ample time for the journey out and back.

By land there are several road entry points from Algeria, while the Trans-Maghreb Railway links Morocco and Algeria with Tunisia.

Customs

In the airport arrival hall, while you are waiting for luggage, check the Duty-Free shop which offers a limited choice of liquor and cigarettes. You can buy duty-free's before passing through Customs control. Typical price for a one-litre bottle of Teacher's whisky is £4. Cigarettes are principally the well-known American brands, and French favourites like Gitanes and Gauloises. If you cannot live without your favourite brand of Scotch, remember that Tunisian bar prices for imported drinks are very high. So take the normal one-litre duty-free quota before departure from Britain. The cigarette limit is 400.

On entry, articles such as cassette recorders, electronic goods and portable computers may be noted by the Customs in your passport. On departure, keep these items as hand luggage, to show the Customs officials that the equipment hasn't been sold off as unauthorized imports. If you cannot produce the goods, there'll be something to pay.

Import and export of Tunisian currency is strictly prohibited. Foreign currency import is unlimited, subject to declaration when the amount exceeds the equivalent of £500. All currency documentation (exchange receipts) should be retained.

Reconversion of local currency into foreign currency on departure is up to 30% of sums exchanged, as shown on exchange receipts, but with a top limit of 100 Tunisian Dinars. In theory, airport exchange offices stay open from 7 a.m. until departure of the day's last flight. In practice, it's best to ensure that you have only minimal Tunisian cash by the time you reach the airport. If you arrive close to departure time, it's maddening to find a long, slow queue at the exchange desk. Tunisian dinars are not valid in duty-free shops. However, you can always buy just one more woolly camel at the souvenir stores.

Currency

The monetary unit is the Tunisian dinar, which divides into 1000 millimes. The variable rate of exchange, government controlled, is around £1 = 1.6 Dinar. Banknotes are of 1, 5, 10 and 20 Dinars. Mostly, at the banks, you'll get a stack of fives and tens. Always look carefully at the figures, as

ones and fives look very similar. Silver-coloured coins are one dinar, and half a dinar (500 millimes). Copper coins are 100 millimes, 50m, 20m and 10m. The very lightweight 5m pieces aren't worth picking up.

Banking Hours

Bank opening hours are 8.00 - 11.00 hrs, and 14.00 - 16.00 hrs except Saturdays and Sundays. During summer - July, August and September - they open only from 7.30 or 8.00 hrs till 11.00 hrs.

During Ramadan, opening hours are 8.00 - 11.00 hrs, and 13.00 - 14.30 hrs.

In major resorts, some branches open for tourists during more extended hours. You can also change money at the main hotels and authorised travel agencies, but probably at a less attractive exchange rate. Ignore touts who want to change money.

Remember to keep exchange receipts, needed to convert back any surplus dinars on departure.

Traveller cheques or hard currency are readily negotiable. Eurocheques are honoured by Société Tunisienne de Banque; Banque Internationale Arabe de Tunisie; and Union Internationale de Banque.

Credit Cards

Access, Mastercard, Visa and other plastic are accepted wherever you see those credit card signs: in shops, hotels and restaurants, particularly in the main tourist centres. But don't rely too heavily on credit cards. In most places, you can only talk banknotes.

Likewise, don't rely totally on credit cards for getting cash! Particularly in the South, you could waste much time in tracking down a bank branch that accepts your card. Access and Visa are handled by BIAT - Banque Internationale Arabe de Tunisie. They can pay out up to 75 dinars on the spot - about £50. If you need more, up to £350 per day, you pay 4 dinars and wait an hour, while they telephone for authority to make the payment.

Have your passport ready, in case the cashier wants to check your face and signature. When the debit reaches your account, the total is converted at the day's dinar exchange rate as quoted in the *Financial Times*. For cash advances, interest is charged from the day the money is taken, until full repayment is made. You can avoid interest by depositing enough cash in your credit-card account before departure.

At shops of the Office Nationale de l'Artisanat, there's a 10% discount on purchases of over 50 dinars, if you pay in hard currency or traveller cheques; or 5% discount on credit cards. Worth remembering, if you suddenly want to buy a carpet!

Always take precautions in case you lose your card. Keep a separate note of your credit-card numbers. Report loss immediately to any bank displaying the appropriate symbol. Your maximum loss is then limited, following the rules of your credit-card company.

WC problems

You have to be desperate, to use the facilities in the average town café. Sometimes the gap between utter misery and fulfillment is measured by a few sheets of toilet paper. Always carry a few spare sheets in your holdall, in case of emergencies.

News

The London newspapers arrive spasmodically in the principal resorts a day or two after publication. Typical newspaper prices are one dinar for the heavy dailies; 1,700 TD for the posh Sundays; 700 millimes for the tabloids.

There are six local daily newspapers - two in Arabic, four in French - but there is no English-language journal.

On TV, Channel One transmits in Arabic only; Channel Two offers 3½ hours' in French. There is a similar split between the National and International Channels of Tunisian Radio.

If your holiday would be ruined without important home news like up-to-date Test Match scores, it's worth travelling with a short-wave radio, to pick up the regular on-the-hour news bulletins of the BBC World Service. Reception varies according to time and location. Try the following wave-lengths:

Early morning - 9410 on 31-meter band; 7185 on 41m band; 6195 on 49m band;

Day-time - 21710 on 13m band; 17705 on 16m band; 15070 on 19m band.

Evening - 12095 kHz on 25m band; 11785 on 25m band; 7325 on 41m band;

Reception on medium or long wave cannot be relied upon, but you could always try your luck on 639 or 1323.

Time

For most of the year, Tunisia is one hour ahead of UK Time, or six hours ahead of America's Eastern Standard Time.

British war cemeteries

As a reminder of the human cost of

123

the North African campaign, cemeteries are located at Beja, 105 kms west of Tunis; at Oued Zarga 80 kms west of Tunis; Massicault along the main highway north of Tunis; Enfidaville, 48 kms north of Sousse; Medjez el Bab, 61 kms west of Tunis; Sfax, south of Sfax, on the Gabès road; Tabarka, 140 kms west of Tunis; at Ras Jebel; at Thibar Seminar 123 kms west of Tunis; Bizerta, 64 kms north of Tunis.

Sexual harassment

Just like in other Mediterranean countries, young bloods fancy themselves as wolves in sheik's clothing. Many are convinced that unaccompanied foreign females have come solely because of Arab reputation for sexual prowess. They don't want to leave anyone disappointed, and approach anyone who seems likely game. In crowded souks, foreign women are liable to be petted and pawed. It's an irritation, like mosquitoes, but not threatening. Just ignore it, or snarl. Better to stay in a group, and avoid 'provocative' clothing when in public places. In the South, a woman should not travel alone.

The Evil-Camera Eye

In the coastal resorts, local people are accustomed to tourists with their desire to point cameras in every direction. Inland, country folk are less tolerant of any invasion of their privacy. In a similar way, most Brits would be angry if Japanese tourists pointed cameras over the garden gate or into a half-open door.

However, if you don't make a big production of it, you can still get colourful shots of Tunisians in costume. Position yourself by a city gate or in a crowded market. With a wide-angle lens for close-up, or long-focus lens for more distant shots, you can get all your pictures without irritating anyone.

In craft workshops, open to tourists, photography is usually OK if you ask permission. Take a flashgun for difficult light conditions in the bazaars. You'll also need it for folklore shows and belly-dancers.

Pack a light cassette recorder, and capture those evocative Tunisian sounds: the call of the muezzin; the beating of drums at a folklore show; the grunting of a camel and the screams of its passenger.

Film prices are higher than in Britain or USA, so take plenty. If you use a specialised film, rather than the standard Kodak or Agfa, then take an over-supply. Off-beat films are hard to find.

Guides

Official licensed guides adhere to a fixed tariff. The local tourist office can make arrangements. Otherwise, in tourist spots you're likely to be accosted by charming youths or schoolkids who want to practise English, and offer to show you around. These would-be guides are usually expecting to be paid, even if they offer their services as a friendly gesture. Their expectations - like their expertise - are often greatly over-rated. Usually, self-appointed guides can do little more than just point to a site, and perhaps tell you its name. No more basic details can be expected. If you do wish to be led around, fix a modest price first.

Another friendly guide service is offered by young men in the bazaars of Tunis. You'll find yourself being led into a carpet or souvenir shop of their choice. The need to cover their commission will severely reduce your bargaining power.

Mosque etiquette

When visiting mosques, the rule is that no shorts are to be worn, and shoulders must be covered. Non-Moslems are allowed only into the courtyard. There is no admittance to prayer halls, though you can usually peep inside. Avoid treading on the mats by the prayer-hall entrances.

Rip-offs

On the beach, watch out for the orange rip-off, or the doughnut lark. The orange man pulls an orange apart and gives it to you as though it's a present, but then demands a high price once you've eaten it. The doughnut man follows the same technique, with high prices.

In currency, look carefully at your coins. The Tunisian dinar looks very much like the UK 10p piece. Also, watch out that you're not given a one-dinar note instead of a five. The one's are slightly smaller, but same colour.

The age-old three-card trick still flourishes in Tunisia. The rules are just the same as at Epsom race course: the punter *always* loses.

Sun and health

Deep suntan is often regarded as being healthy, but doctors now advise caution against overdoing it, because of skin-cancer risk. Against sunburn, the standard advice is well enough known. But many holidaymakers don't fully realise the power of the North African sun, especially if there's a cooling sea breeze.

Take the sun in very small doses for the first few days of a holiday. Use plenty of suntan lotion, reapplied every hour or so after you've been in the pool or sea. Beware of iced drinks while sun-bathing, and then jumping in the pool. Your tummy is bound to rebel. Wash fruit carefully, and consume any drinks before the ice-cubes have dissolved. Most upsets are caused by too much unaccustomed spicy food, or cold beers and bottles of wine.

Tipping

Tunisian salaries are low, so don't forget the waiters, chambermaids or room-boys. Ask your travel-agency rep for guidance on how much. You'll be expected to tip for many quite minor services. In restaurants, a service charge is added on the bill, but it's still normal to leave something extra. With the modest prices for food and drinks, 10% doesn't hurt.

Telephone

Phone calls to UK cost about 5.5 dinars for 3 minutes. There could be a half-hour wait if you are phoning from the hotel. It's cheaper to dial yourself at one dinar a minute from PTT post offices. The silver-coloured long distance payphones accept half-dinar and one-dinar coins.

Wait for dial tone and insert a coin. Then dial 00 44 for Britain (00 1 for USA or Canada), followed by area code without the first zero, and the number. A display shows when to insert more coins. Keep the slot well fed, and any excess coins will be returned when the receiver is replaced.

What to Pack

It depends what season you are travelling. In high summer, the bare minimum of beachwear and lightweight clothing is enough, with a jacket for the cooler evenings of September and October. In spring and autumn, add a sweater or two and a raincoat. In winter months, be prepared with brolly and topcoat for showers and cool days.

Unless you're staying at luxury-grade hotels, you'll need only a minimal amount of formal wear, like a necktie. For sightseeing of mosques, 'decent' clothing is required, such as a pair of trousers. For tramping around classical sites or cobbled souks, take sensible walking shoes or trainers.

Take your full needs of sun-tan lotion, medicaments and toiletries. Pack 'Wet Ones' - moist tissues for instant cleanups. Fifty large wipes in a dispenser are great when you are feeling hot and sweaty on a desert safari.

Public Holidays

January 1 - New Year's Day

March 20 - Independence Day

April 9 - Martyrs Day

Martyrs Day

May 1 - Labour Day

July 25 - Republic Day

August 13 - Women's Day

Moslem Religious Feastdays

These vary according to the Hegira religious calendar, and move forward by 10 or 11 days each year. For 1990, the dates are:

Ramadan - from 27 March to 26 April.

Aid Essighir - celebrates the end of Ramadan - 26 April.

Aid El Kebir - the Mutton Festival - 2 July.

New Year's Day Hegirian Calendar - 23 July.

Mouled - the Prophet Mohammed's birthday - 1 October.

Electricity

220-volt AC almost everywhere in Tunisia, using continental style 2-pin plugs. Pack an appropriate plug adaptor for any appliances you take.

TOP TRAVEL TITLES FROM SETTLE PRESS

The following books all feature in the highly popular WHERE TO GO IN series, recommended by Thomson Holidays.

WHERE TO GO IN GREECE
by Trevor Webster
An up-to-date, easy-to-read, illustrated guide to the islands and mainland centres.

"an exceptional title for both those seeking culture and the sun". *The Bookseller*

£5.99 paper 0907070264
3rd reprint 1986
(Revised Edition)

☐

CORFU AND THE IONIAN ISLANDS
by Trevor Webster
Travellers are offered a modern Garden of Eden with Trevor Webster as their personal guide.

£9.99 hard 0907070329
£6.99 paper 0907070272
featuring 32 pages of full colour: reprint 1989

☐
☐

RHODES AND THE DODECANESE ISLANDS
by Trevor Webster
The appeal and atmosphere of Rhodes and the nearby islands, including tiny Kassos and Symi with its stunning harbour are brought to life.

£9.99 hard 0907070353
£6.99 paper 0907070310
featuring 32 pages of full colour: publication 1987

☐
☐

ATHENS, MAINLAND AND THE NORTH AEGEAN ISLANDS
by Trevor Webster
Trevor Webster takes the reader on a magic tour of Athens, the mainland and over twenty islands.

£9.99 hard 0907070337
£6.99 paper 0907070280
Featuring 32 pages of colour
Publication 1986

☐
☐

CRETE AND THE CYCLADES ISLANDS
by Trevor Webster
Crete and the Cyclades are islands of great colour, character and contrast. The atmosphere of their stupendous mountains, beaches, harbours and history is relayed by Trevor Webster.

£9.99 hard 0907070388
£6.99 paper 0907070396
Publication 1987

☐
☐

WHERE TO GO IN SPAIN
A guide to the Iberian peninsula
by H. Dennis-Jones
Includes rating guides for all the Spanish coastal regions and colourful descriptions of the interior.

£9.99 hard 0907070426
£5.99 paper 0907070434
1987

☐
☐

WHERE TO GO IN THE CANARY ISLANDS
by Reg Butler
Depending on what you want from a holiday – jetset nightlife, or peace-and-quiet; energetic sport or an inch-deep suntan; dramatic scenery or city sightseeing and shopping – Where To Go In The Canary Islands can help you choose which island can best fill your requirements.

£14.00 hard 0907070671
£8.99 paper 090707068X
1990

☐
☐

WHERE TO GO IN TUNISIA
by Reg Butler
While most visitors choose Tunisia for its year-round Mediterranean sunshine, the book also describes the fascination of Roman remains, Islamic cities, country markets, oases and Berber strongholds.

£14.00 hard 0907070485
£8.99 paper 0907070493
1990

☐
☐

GREEK ISLAND DELIGHTS
by Trevor Webster
Trevor Webster, best selling author of Where To Go in Greece continues to explore both the tourist resorts and those hidden away spots on the 12 of the most popular and magical isles in Greece. These are Crete, Corfu, Rhodes, Kos, Samos, Skiathos, Mykonos, Santorini, Paros, Thassos, Kephalonia and Zakynthos.

£14.00 hard 0907070604
£8.99 paper 0907070612

☐
☐

CITY BREAKS SERIES (Started in 1989 in association with Thomson Holidays)

The following books form part of a brand new concept in entertaining guidebooks for shortstay visitors. Each book is absolutely up-to-date and revised editions are planned for *each* year. All are a convenient wallet shaped 200 x 100 mm and include maps/illustrations together with many personal tips and recommendations on what not to miss both in the cities and surrounding areas.

PARIS 1990   £3.25 0907070639   ☐
by Reg Butler
The pleasures of Paris, capital of capitals, are spread out for incurable romantics, art lovers, sightseers and a host of travellers with other special interests. City Breaks Paris is also your personal guide to a selection of recommended bars, restaurants and nightspots.

AMSTERDAM 1990   £3.25 0907070647   ☐
by Reg Butler
Reg Butler is an enchanting guide to a city of canals, contrasts and surprises, that offers a dozen different holidays for the short stay visitor.

ROME, VENICE & FLORENCE 1990   £3.25 0907070663   ☐
by Reg Butler
Rome, Venice, Florence – How to choose? Each has its individual charm and charisma. This book provides you with the personal 'inside view' and ensures you do not miss out on any aspect whatever your taste.

MOSCOW/LENINGRAD 1990   £3.25 0907070655   ☐
by Reg Butler
With the new spirit of *Glasnost*, the Soviet Union is becoming an ever-more-popular destination for western visitors. Learn the Russian ABC, ride the Metro, stroll around the Kremlin, attend morning service in a Russian orthodox monastery, go shop-gazing along Leningrad's famous Nevsky Prospekt – this guidebook is packed with advice on finding your way around.

ISTANBUL 1990   £3.25 090707054X   ☐
by Reg Butler
Visit two continents in one Citybreak. This guide to Istanbul covers both sides of the Bosphorus, where soaring bridges link Europe and Asia. Author Reg Butler has visited Istanbul every year since 1950, and can be your step-by-step guide to one of Europe's most fascinating and historic cities.

Buy them at your local bookshops or send in this coupon to

SETTLE PRESS (Reader Service Dept.)
10 Boyne Terrace Mews, London W11 3LR

Please send me the book(s) I have ticked. I am enclosing £
(prices cover postage and handling in UK).

Mr/Mrs/Miss . . . .

Address . . . .

. . . .

. . . .

Sousse –
Plenty of choice for an
open-air lunch

Monastir
In the colourful Medina

Port El Kantaoui
Enjoying a meal beside
the Marina

Thomson

No. **1** *for* **Holidays** *to* **Tunisia**

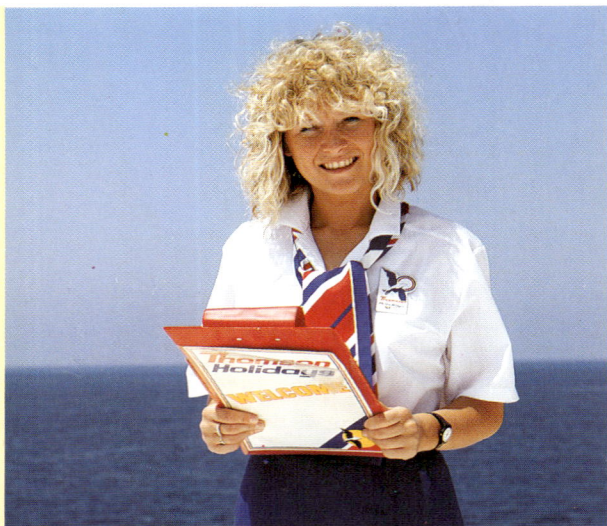

No. **1** for choice – the best range of resorts, local airports to fly from, and types of accommodation on offer.

No. **1** for value – Thomson consistently voted the No. 1 by Travel Agents every year since 1982.

No. **1** for reliability – the security of travelling with Britain's largest holiday company.

No wonder that, wherever they go, more and more people choose Thomson, Britain's No. 1 holiday company.

Choose your kind of holiday from these exciting Thomson brochures, available from your travel agent

Summer Sun Winter Sun

Hotel-based holidays in Monastir, Port El Kantaoui, Hammamet and Sousse.

Family C·H·O·I·C·E

Family Holidays with Thomson Big T Club and Little T Club for children.

A LA CARTE

Holidays of distinction: four and five star hotels with complimentary flowers and wine on arrival.

A T YOUNG HEART

Unbeatable value for the over 55's.

AIR FARES

Low cost Air Fares for the independent traveller.